WHAT PEOPLE ARE SAYING ABOUT

Thriving on the Jagged Edge

When we heard Max's story and read his book, we knew we had to have him on the show.

—JULIE BLIM
PRODUCER, *700 CLUB*

Max Davis' insights are real, having been forged on the hard anvil of life. You will be both challenged and inspired by his message.

—RICHARD EXLEY
AUTHOR, CONFERENCE LEADER, AND PASTOR

Max Davis is a passionate communicator who writes and speaks from the heart to reach the heart. By exposing the scars of his own life and others, he reveals the healing power of Christ. Thriving on the Jagged Edge is a must-read for any-one who finds himself facing challenging circumstances.

—RON NEWCOMB
SINGLES YOUNG ADULT DIRECTOR,
MCLEAN BIBLE CHURCH, MCLEAN, VA

THRIVING
ON THE JAGGED
EDGE

ALSO BY MAX DAVIS

Desperate Dependence

THRIVING
ON THE JAGGED
EDGE

LIVE ABOVE YOUR CIRCUMSTANCES

MAX DAVIS

LIFE JOURNEY®

Bringing Home the Message for Life

COOK COMMUNICATIONS MINISTRIES
Colorado Springs, Colorado • Paris, Ontario
KINGSWAY COMMUNICATIONS LTD
Eastbourne, England

Life Journey® is an imprint of
Cook Communications Ministries, Colorado Springs, CO 80918
Cook Communications, Paris, Ontario
Kingsway Communications, Eastbourne, England

THRIVING ON THE JAGGED EDGE

Author's note: I have utilized in this work several portions from one of my previous books, *It's Only a Flat Tire in the Rain,* which is no longer in print. The sections used have been significantly revised and expanded.

Cover Design: Two Moore Designs/Ray Moore
Cover Photo Credit: ©BigStock Photo

Published in association with the literary agency of Mark Gilroy Communications, 6528 E. 101st St., Ste. 416, Tulsa, OK 74133-6754.

The Web addresses (URLs) recommended throughout this book are solely offered as a resource to the reader. The citation of these Web sites does not in any way imply an endorsement on the part of the author or the publisher, nor does the author or publisher vouch for their content for the life of this book.

First Printing, 2006
Printed in Canada

1 2 3 4 5 6 7 8 9 10 Printing/Year 10 09 08 07 06

ISBN-13: 978-0-7814-4276-3
ISBN-10: 0-7814-4276-1

LCCN: 2005937773

To Gerald and Sharon:
I would never have had this ministry
if it hadn't been for you.
You guys are a blessing. I love you!

CONTENTS

Acknowledgments

This is my fourth book and, as was the case with each one before, there is a plethora of people to thank. This time, however, I would like to express gratitude to five special people who have greatly influenced my life and career.

Mary McNeil: More than the world's best editor, in so many ways you've been a gentle and kind teacher, and of course, a friend. Thanks for your honest feedback and your support. I appreciate it! Working with you has made me a better writer and a better person.

Richard Exley: From afar and up close you will never know how much you have encouraged and inspired me. Thanks for being an awesome writer, a good listener, and a dear friend.

Larry Koenig: You, too, have been a friend and sounding board. Thanks for enduring all the whining sessions over lunch. So many times when I was down, out, and on the verge of giving up, a word from you got me back on track again. Let's not stop the tradition.

Mark Gilroy: What can I say? Thanks for *always* making time for me in your busy schedule, for continuing to believe in my writing abilities, and for enduring with me as I paid my dues. You are a blessing, friend, and a great agent!

My wife, Alanna: With each book it's the same— you're a warrior, a partner in the trenches, an encourager, and a solid rock in my life. There's no way I could do what I do without you. I love you so much. Of all my friends, you're the best!

The Jagged Edge

If we chose what was going to happen to
us, we would never grow.

—Mark Sanbor

Dave Solosky* leaned forward in his Toyota Camry, straining to see the taillights of the car in front of him. Though his windshield wipers flapped wildly on high, they cleared the glass for only a split second with each swipe. He thought about pulling over and waiting until the storm slackened, but he really wanted

* Fictional name

to get home. Besides, Dave had made this commute hundreds of times. So he just gripped the wheel a little tighter and continued across the Atchafalaya Basin Bridge on I-10 heading out of Baton Rouge, Louisiana, toward his home in Lafayette.

Glancing in his rearview mirror, Dave was stunned to see an eighteen-wheeler bearing down on him. Then, despite the torrential rain, the driver of the big rig moved to the outside lane of the interstate and began to make his way around. As he pulled abreast of Dave's car, the huge tires sent a blinding sheet of water cascading over the Toyota. Unable to see even the truck's taillights, Dave fought to maintain control of his car. A sudden thud and jolt left Dave wondering whether the truck had veered into him or he into the truck. Regardless, his car was now hydroplaning out of control, and his concentrated attempts at straightening it out were useless. Dave braced himself for the inevitable just before he slammed into the concrete railing that lined the bridge. For an instant it seemed his car would plunge into the murky swamp some forty feet below, carrying him to almost certain death. Miraculously it did not. Instead, it teetered treacherously on the bridge's jagged edge.

Stunned from the impact, Dave took a moment to get his bearings. Between the air bag in his face and the pelting rain, he was virtually blind. He sensed his predicament was perilous. The wind continued whipping, making the car rock and screech against the barrier. Dave knew he needed to get out—and quickly!

After carefully unbuckling the seat belt, he feverishly attempted to open the driver's side door, but it wouldn't budge. Sliding over to the passenger's door, he pushed it, only to discover that it was wedged against the railing. Another gust of wind caused the car to rock, sending Dave into a panic. He frantically kicked out the door window and pulled himself out of the car, oblivious to the jagged shards of glass that cut him. Seemingly out of nowhere, a hand clutched his, pulling him the rest of the way out. Once he emerged, Dave collapsed against the car of the motorist who had stopped to help. He had suffered only minor injuries, and a wrecker was able to winch his vehicle off the railing. Dave said he was painfully aware throughout his ordeal that at any moment the car could have plunged headlong into the swamp, sending him to an early grave.

STRESS STORMS

Does your life ever resemble Dave's drive home? Do torrential rains of discouragement seem to fall on you? Are you feeling blinded by pressures that never seem to let up? Are you struggling just to stay on the road? Do you ever feel like you're hanging on the jagged edge, that at any moment you might drop into the

murky swamp of despair? We live in turbulent times—
a fluctuating economy, out-of-control crime, disease
and disaster, financial pressure, job dissatisfaction,
school shootings, employment layoffs, broken relationships, seemingly universal misunderstanding, and
increasing worry over wayward children. Stress has
become the norm in our society.

Then there's that nagging little thing called
pain. Joseph Parker, one of history's great ministers,
once said to a group of young seminary students,
"Preach to the suffering and you
will never lack a congregation.
There's a broken heart in every
pew."[1] People throughout the
world today are hurting and
stressed for myriad reasons. We all
long to live in peace and fulfillment, to experience the abundant
life that Jesus talked about. Most
of us, however, find ourselves in a
brutal, nerve-racking struggle for
survival.

Sometimes it's all we can do
to put one foot in front of the
other and keep trudging forward.
On such days we're not interested
in the *Ten Secrets to Wealth* or the *Five Steps to
Winning Big*. Success in such times consists simply

EVEN THOUGH
WE'RE LIVING
ON THE JAGGED
EDGE, WE CAN
DO MORE THAN
MERELY SUR-
VIVE; WE CAN
ACTUALLY
THRIVE!

of getting through the stress and pain of the moment to a place where we can experience a degree of peace.

As an author and speaker, I find myself frequently lecturing on the topic of pain and adversity. Like most people, I've had my share of storms to weather. You've heard it said, "Write about what you know," and it seems my whole career has been "forged on the hard anvil of life." All of my previous books were birthed out of personal struggles.

I don't claim to be some sort of guru with all the answers. But my personal experiences, as well as the struggles of other people, have taught me a thing or two. One lesson is this: Even though we're living on the jagged edge, we can do more than merely survive; we can actually thrive!

BEYOND SURVIVAL

What do I mean by the term "thriving on the jagged edge"? Thriving is not some superficial notion that seeks to minimize our heartrending pains or overwhelming circumstances. Neither is it about material success. It's about trusting God and experiencing *soulfulness*, which I'll discuss later, in the midst of life's most difficult trials. Thrivers live within the reality of their pain and unanswered questions, but they have also come to trust God's

faithfulness. They know His peace and His supernatural staying power that enables them to live life
fully despite their struggles.

Thriving on the jagged edge is not about denying reality; it's about responding to reality while
affirming a greater eternal reality. Elisabeth Kubler-
Ross wrote, "When circumstances are at their worst,
we can find our best."[2] We might also add, "When
circumstances are at their worst, we can find God's
best." It's on the jagged edge of epidemics that we
discover new vaccines. It's on the jagged edge of
need that we innovate and invent. It's on the jagged
edge of tribulation that heroes are made. It's on the
jagged edge of adversity that God does His greatest
and most miraculous work in us. If we never had to
face any Goliaths in our lives, we would never know
God's power to deliver and sustain us.

THE THREE DAUGHTERS

Nancy Kay Rodgers and Carol Bradshaw are shining
examples of thriving on the jagged edge. Nancy Kay
lost her twenty-year-old daughter, Leigh Ann, in a
boating accident. Then on Nancy's birthday in 2000,
she lost her thirty-six-year-old daughter, Melissa, from
a tragic pregnancy-related complication. The child
Melissa was carrying also died. Nancy's friend Carol
Bradshaw endured the loss of her twenty-year-old

daughter, Lindsay, on Mother's Day, 1999, in an automobile accident.

The grief these two women experienced is barely within reach of our imagination. But instead of giving in to the relentless tug of bitterness and anger that threatened to drag them into the dark pit of hopelessness, Nancy and Carol chose to abandon themselves to the open arms of their compassionate heavenly Father. As God embraced them, He also filled them with the power to thrive instead of merely survive. Out of tragedy God birthed the Three Daughters Gift Shop on Main Street in Saluda, South Carolina.

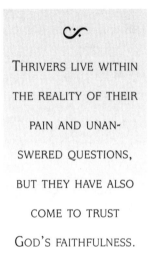

THRIVERS LIVE WITHIN THE REALITY OF THEIR PAIN AND UNANSWERED QUESTIONS, BUT THEY HAVE ALSO COME TO TRUST GOD'S FAITHFULNESS.

No one who walks into the quaint, beautifully decorated shop with the aroma of coffee wafting through the air would ever suspect that the two women behind the counter are there as a result of losing their three daughters.

"Opening the shop is a ministry we are providing with divine guidance," Nancy told me.

The store came into being because of Nancy and Carol's friendship and their desire to remember the spirit of their beautiful daughters Leigh Ann, Melissa, and Lindsay.

"We missed shopping with our daughters. Shopping was not fun anymore, and there was no one to fill that void," they told me. "So we opened the shop in their memory as a place of refuge for people. People come in just to read or drink coffee. Sometimes teachers come in to sit and grade papers."

> WHEN CIRCUM-
> STANCES ARE
> AT THEIR
> WORST, WE
> CAN FIND
> GOD'S BEST.

Each day folks stop in and ask, "Who are the 'Three Daughters'?" Carol said, "We're amazed at how many times we share our story."

The Three Daughters Gift Shop is also the headquarters for the Saluda branch of Angel Touch Ministry, a mentoring organization to parents who have lost children.

"We realized how much the parents need to share and just talk," Nancy said. "We've seen that as we lifted a hand to help others, we were lifting ourselves, because we've been there, and we know their pain. We want to bring hope that they, too, will make it."

Nancy and Carol visit parents who have lost a child and give them a gift bag filled with a devotional book, a book on dealing with grief, and an angel necklace.

"We've gone to comfort total strangers before," said Nancy. "But they instantly know we feel what they're going through. Our times of sorrow equip us to minister to others. God expects us to learn something from every circumstance, including grief."

Carol added, "Reaching out to others with compassion and comfort in their time of need and using our experiences and understanding is what God asked us to do. We know without a doubt that the love we shared with our daughters was God's everlasting gift."

What an encouraging story! If God can do that for Nancy and Carol, He will surely do it for us in our unique ordeals. For sure, life is not all sugar and spice. You certainly won't get any argument from me about that. Just as Nancy and Carol know, I have learned that life's jagged edges are sharp! They cut into deeply held beliefs and slice through our faith. They stick and poke and make life uncomfortable, sometimes unbearable. Still, we need not live a listless, purposeless existence. We can be fully alive, experiencing God's grace and peace amid all the negatives that surround us.

"YOUR SON IS DEAF"

I remember with vivid precision the day the doctor said the following words: "I'm sorry, Mr. and Mrs. Davis, your son is deaf."

"What?" I replied. "*Deaf!*" I sat there stunned. Numbness stole over me. Then, as the word began to sink into my being, all sorts of emotions ran through my mind. "James *can't* be deaf!" I shouted at the doctor. At that time, all I knew of deafness was those people who chased me down in the supermarket parking lot, handing me cards that read, *I'm deaf; please help me by buying a key chain.* I always felt sorry for them.

"I assure you, your son is deaf," the doctor replied. "We'll need to run more tests to determine the severity of his hearing loss. But he *is* deaf."

James was thirteen months old. Up to that point, he had seemed like a normal toddler: walking, cooing, and laughing. But he had not yet started to talk. When I commented to others about James' late speech development, they usually told me not to worry, that a boy's speech sometimes develops a little more slowly than a girl's. These sentiments temporarily put me at ease because I didn't want to think anything was seriously wrong with my wonderful little boy. Besides, James had been getting regular checkups and had always come back with a clean bill of health.

Then at church one day, James' nursery worker told me I might need to get his ears checked; she had called his name and he hadn't responded. We made an appointment with an ear specialist, expecting to hear the physician say, "James has an infection. Give him this antibiotic and come back in two weeks. He'll be fine." You can imagine our shock when he said those dreadful words, "I'm sorry, but your son is deaf."

That day in the hospital with James, my life and the lives of my family irrevocably changed. Subsequent tests have revealed that James is profoundly deaf. For all practical purposes, he has no hearing at all. He might pick up certain low tones, but only if they're magnified to around 120 decibels—as loud as a jet engine at takeoff. Hearing aids don't help him much.

Leaving the doctor's office that day, I felt as if the weight of the whole world had been dropped onto my shoulders. We drove to our pastor's house. He and his wife sat with us on their sofa as we wept. Later that night, at home, I sneaked up behind James and yelled at the top of my lungs. No response. He didn't even realize I was there. I wept some more. I wept for days.

God answers prayer. I believe that. I've witnessed dramatic answers to prayer. But when I prayed for James, all I felt was a cold silence. Others prayed on his behalf. Whole congregations offered prayers. No response. For weeks I clanged pots and pans around

> OUR TIMES OF SORROW EQUIP US TO MINISTER TO OTHERS.

James, hoping for some reaction from him, some sign of hearing. But there was nothing. Pain and guilt dominated my emotions: If I had been more observant, maybe we could have caught his condition earlier. What if I had lived a better life and been more holy? Some insensitive Christians even implied that if we had had more faith, this tragic event would not have occurred.

My entire family was instantly thrust into a world we had no desire to enter—the world of the deaf. I realized that James would never hear my voice, the sound of a bird chirping, or music playing. My chest felt as if it were going to explode with pain. My personal passions were playing the guitar and singing, but all my desire for performing music left. How could I play when James would never be able to share it with me?

> WE CAN BE FULLY ALIVE, EXPERIENCING GOD'S GRACE AND PEACE AMID ALL THE NEGATIVES THAT SURROUND US.

Stepping into this new world forced me to confront some intensely uncomfortable issues. Think about it. A deaf person cannot speak on the telephone or even answer the doorbell without some kind of aid. His communication and socialization is extremely limited because he can communicate only by sign language or through an interpreter. As you might imagine, learning sign language is not high on the priority list for most people. To be deaf is akin to living in a strange country where people speak an unknown language. Because the deaf have to memorize words from pictures or grasp a definition from body language and gestures, their vocabulary tends to be limited. It's difficult for a deaf person to grasp the meanings of abstract words such as *manifest, manipulation,* or *sovereignty.* As a result, many deaf people do not realize their full career potential.

These thoughts whirled around in my head along with questions that haunted me: *Who will James marry? How will he support himself? Will he reach his full potential as a person?* The list of questions seemed endless.

Entering the world of the deaf meant years of sign language classes for all of us and a special school for James when he was only eighteen months old. In his most formative years, it was imperative that he learn to communicate.

THIS PRESENT PAIN

Sixteen years have passed since James was diagnosed as deaf. Sixteen tough years. It's common knowledge in the deaf community that experts say raising one deaf child is equivalent to raising several hearing children. You might expect me to write, "Over the years I've come to see deafness as a wonderful gift, and life is great now." The truth is, I still struggle with James' deafness. He's now seventeen and is reading on a third-grade level. Yet he is as bright as any other seventeen-year-old and holds the same dreams and desires as any hearing teenager.

My son's deafness has been one of the sharpest jagged edges this life has handed me. Each day brings new challenges. There is no pain like the pain of seeing your child suffer. And it never goes away. It is present in every activity, at every waking hour. When I sleep, it is there. When I wake, it is there. I never have a day when the pain is completely gone. It's like a sore toe that refuses to heal, and I have no choice but to accept the fact that it will be sore the rest of my life. I've just learned to protect it as best I can and then live with it.

James will soon be eighteen years old. He and I were recently eating out when he signed to me, "I don't want to be deaf. I've asked God again and again and again to give me hearing, but nothing has happened." I then told James through my tears that I would give him my hearing if I could, but I couldn't. The pain of James' situation is still an ever-present reality. I would give up my hearing in a split second if it meant James would receive his.

TRANSCENDENT HOPE

There remains yet another truth we must grasp: There is hope! But our hope lies not in our ability to prevent pain from touching our lives nor in our ability to control circumstances. Rather, it is nestled in the fact that we can have peace during tough times, and we can transcend those periods, regardless of their intensity. The Merriam-Webster dictionary defines *transcend* as "to rise above."[3] Notice that *transcend* does not mean "to eliminate." Trials will always be part of the human experience. They come in myriad fashions, at different levels and in different intensities. This book, however, presents principles that, when applied to our individual lives, will help us to do more than merely exist.

Now, you may be thinking, *You don't have a clue what I'm going through. I'm angry, bitter, and numb. You talk about thriving, but I'm not interested in thriving. I just want to die.* My answer to you is, "No, I don't know what it's like to go through your particular situation, but God does. He sees you and feels your pain, and I still say there is hope."

This book is not about magic formulas and quick fixes. In the following pages, you'll meet real people—inspiring people—who are living in the trenches and who are making their lives count despite their difficulties. My prayer is that this book will serve as a tool to spur you to rugged and courageous action; that it will help you hold on until the sunlight pierces the darkness and your path clears; that it will stimulate you to step out and make the changes that are necessary for you to begin walking in your God-ordained purpose. Regardless of your stage along life's journey, this book can help. Enjoy the read, and may you *thrive on the jagged edge!*

The Myth
of the
"Normal" Life

☙

*Life is difficult, and difficulty is
the only path to wisdom.*

—David Jeremiah

The preceding quote from David Jeremiah is a
hard pill to swallow. It's hard because we want life to
be painless, without a struggle. We desire a "normal"
life. The problem is, our definition of *normal* is often
distorted. For most of us a normal life means a
smooth ride—a life of happiness and ease. To make
matters worse, our materialistic society constantly
bombards us with images that market unrealistic

expectations. It sells us the idea that in order to be happy we must have this thing, live in that house, look like a supermodel, be *married* to a supermodel (or super-hunk), and live in the suburbs with two perfect kids. You get the picture. Hollywood-inspired ideals lead us to believe that a normal life overflows with excess and that if we don't possess all these things or if we have problems, then we are abnormal or we did something to deserve our difficulties. Even other Christians sometimes make us feel that way. We then fall into the trap of comparing our lives to theirs, and we are often oblivious to their personal struggles. For the most part, we see only the surface of other people's lives. Only when we look beyond Sunday morning smiles do we discover them to be fellow strugglers.

> OUR QUEST FOR NORMAL DRIVES THE WAY WE THINK LIFE SHOULD BE, CAUSING US TO MEASURE OURSELVES AGAINST UNREALISTIC STANDARDS.

Despite this reality, our quest for normal drives the way we think life should be, causing us to measure ourselves against unrealistic standards. Then when adversity hits or our plans don't pan out, we feel cheated—as if this were not normal, that we are the exception. This is one reason why we commonly respond to difficult circumstances by asking, "Why me?" It's because we think life's jagged edges are not really supposed to happen to us, that they are abnormal. Which leads us to the next question: What is a normal life?

STORMY WEATHER

Scott Peck wrote in his classic book, *The Road Less Traveled*, "Life is difficult. This is a great truth, one of the greatest truths. It is a great truth because once we truly see this truth, we transcend it. Once we truly know that life is difficult—once we truly understand and accept it—then life is no longer difficult."[1]

My good friend and author Richard Exley wrote, "No one is immune. In one form or another trouble comes to every one of us. Do what you will, you cannot avoid it. You may minimize your risks, but there is no escaping it. Some people spend enormous amounts of time and energy, not to mention money, in a desperate attempt to keep it at bay, but in the end they discover that there is no avoiding it. It is inevitable—sooner or later trouble comes to us all."[2]

The apostle Peter guaranteed that difficulties are the norm when he wrote, "Dear friends, do not be surprised at the painful trial you are suffering, as

though something strange were happening to you"
(1 Peter 4:12).

Jesus said it this way: "I have told you these
things, so that in me you may have peace. In this
world you will have trouble" (John 16:33). The
Greek word translated *trouble* in this verse is *thlipsis,*
which means "anguish, affliction, tribulation, pressure, or persecution"[3]—all sorts of problems.

On another occasion Jesus told the story of the
wise and foolish builders.

> Whoever hears these sayings of Mine,
> and does them, I will liken him to a
> wise man who built his house on the
> rock: *and the rain descended, the floods
> came, and the winds blew and beat on
> that house;* and it did not fall, for it was
> founded on the rock. But everyone who
> hears these saying of Mine, and does not
> do them, will be like a foolish man who
> built his house on the sand: and the rain
> descended, the floods came, and the
> winds blew and beat on that house; and
> it fell. And great was its fall. (Matthew
> 7:24–27 NKJV)

Jesus pointed out, though indirectly, that
whether we are wise or foolish, problems are

inevitable. At some point, the storms of life will come and beat on our house. And the storms in this passage were not just some little showers but major winds and floods that pounded on the house, threatening to destroy it. It's important to understand this so that we can not only prepare our foundation beforehand, but so that we don't have to waste time wondering or complaining about why we're facing difficulties.

> ⁓
>
> I HAVE TOLD YOU THESE THINGS, SO THAT IN ME YOU MAY HAVE PEACE. IN THIS WORLD YOU WILL HAVE TROUBLE (JOHN 16:33).

A normal life is one of adversity and struggle, plain and simple. As Scott Peck and David Jeremiah said, life is difficult. People sometimes choose to complain or become resentful because they believe life should not be this way, that their problems are the exception to life's rule. How many times have we made statements such as "Nothing ever comes easily for me" or "Dark clouds seem to follow me wherever I go," implying that others don't experience the same setbacks we do? A woman once said to me, "All my life I've tried to do the right thing, and this is what I get." Her perception of how life should be was different from the reality she was experiencing. She had picked up the notion that if she did "all the right things," her life would be problem free. Consequently, she saw herself as a victim.

VICTIM NO MORE

It's true that we sometimes become genuine victims. Under such circumstances, it's appropriate to take action to protect ourselves and to pursue justice. We do not, however, have to live with a victim mentality. A victim mentality undermines our faith and turns us into people who drain joy from others rather than people who give joy to others.

June Scobee Rogers chose not to adopt a victim mentality. On January 28, 1986, she stood with her son, daughter, and grandbaby, watching in horror and disbelief as the space shuttle *Challenger* exploded before their eyes in the clear blue Florida sky. June's husband and her children's father, Dick Scobee, was one of seven shuttle crew members.

She wrote the following recollection in her book *Silver Linings*:

> I was angry with God for letting this happen. The energy used for anger, hate, and grief were sapping me of my life.

[Then one day, at the end of myself, I cried out to God in desperation], "If you won't take me," I begged, "then give me strength ... to live this life, to help me solve these problems, to overcome these feelings of guilt."

That moment, I became like a child again. I turned my life over to God. God was in control—not I. For the first time in my life since grappling with this loss, I relinquished complete control to God. A joyous Spirit challenged me to live, to accept my problems, to discover new joy in a new life.

Though I was alone in my house, I didn't feel alone. No longer the master of my own fate, the simple innocence of the child I once knew told me that God was with me, in control. The pressure, the anger, the pain, and the guilt slowly drained from my body. A part of me died,

LIFE IS A SERIES OF STRUGGLES. WE BEGIN TO TRANSCEND AND THRIVE ONLY WHEN WE RECOGNIZE THAT TRUTH AND LET GOD MEET US AT OUR POINT OF NEED.

but a stronger, more centered, saner self
was born.

[As time passed] I learned lessons of
forgiveness, overcoming adversity, problem solving, forfeiting control to God,
and the opportunity to welcome new life
through a closer walk with our Savior,
Jesus Christ.

Greatest of all, I learned lessons about
love—the beautiful power of love that
can cause a magnificent phoenix to rise
up out of the ashes of a tragedy.[4]

Life is a series of
struggles. We begin to
transcend and thrive
only when we recognize
that truth and let God
meet us at our point of
need. That realization is
neither negative nor
fatalistic. Was Jesus neg-

A NORMAL LIFE IS ONE OF

ADVERSITY AND STRUGGLE,

PLAIN AND SIMPLE.

ative when He told us that we would have trouble
in our lives? No. He was being realistic about this
fallen and unpredictable world in which we live.
Armed with this understanding, we begin to focus
our faith, prayers, and hope on crafting solutions.

We stop seeing ourselves as victims of life, and, regardless of the depth of our trials, we become like Nancy, Carol, and June: conduits for hope and joy.

We have this treasure in earthen vessels, that the excellence of the power may be of God and not of us. We are hard-pressed on every side, yet not crushed; we are perplexed, but not in despair; persecuted, but not forsaken; struck down, but not destroyed.

2 CORINTHIANS 4:7–9 NKJV

EMBRACING THE STRUGGLE

*Instead of fighting it, we embrace it.
Not masochistically, but in faith believing that what the evil one intended for
our destruction God has redeemed and is
now using for our eternal good.*

—RICHARD EXLEY

Once we understand that life is a struggle, we must put that knowledge into action by embracing the struggle. As I emphasized in chapter 2, this is not a negative frame of mind. It is not about being fatalistic, but about being real. I am an optimist, a faith-driven person. Ours is a God of miracles and answered prayer. As James 5:16 (NKJV) states, "The effective, fervent prayer of a righteous man avails much." Embracing the struggle does not mean we do not seek relief. But while our prayers do avail—or gain—much, God does not always deliver us in the way we hope. He sometimes calls us to walk through the fire. To embrace the struggle simply means to replace the fear of struggle with an ability to see the value in it. Obviously, no one in his or her right mind wishes for struggle and pain. But struggle and pain are facts of life, and what we allow God to do with them makes all the difference. We have a big God. He is able to use the worst and most haphazard circumstances to develop our characters and to further His purposes.

> ONCE WE UNDERSTAND THAT LIFE IS A STRUGGLE, WE MUST PUT THAT KNOWLEDGE INTO ACTION BY EMBRACING THE STRUGGLE.

The great abolitionist Frederick Douglass said, "If there is no struggle, there is no progress."[1] Strength and muscular definition come to the bodybuilder as he increases the resistance in his workout routine. A little chick breaks free of its shell as it struggles to peck its way out. The very struggle we fear is what

builds the strength necessary for survival in the outside world. Shakespeare wrote in *As You Like It,*
"Sweet are the uses of adversity."[2] James 1:2–4 (AB)
says, "Consider it wholly joyful, my brethren, whenever you are enveloped in or encounter trials of any
sort or fall into various temptations. Be assured and
understand that the trial and proving of your faith
bring out endurance and steadfastness and patience.
But let endurance and steadfastness and patience
have full play and do a thorough work, so that you
may be [people] perfectly and fully developed [with
no defects], lacking in nothing."

Was the apostle James actually saying we're to be
happy ("wholly joyful") and ecstatic when we go
through tough times, when we watch our children
suffer, when we're in deep pain? In John 16:33
(NKJV), right after Jesus promised us that in this
world "[we] will have tribulation," He said, "But be
of good cheer, I have overcome the world." Are
Nancy and Carol supposed to be happy and cheer-
ful that their daughters were killed? Am I supposed
to be happy that my son is deaf? That is not what
James and Jesus were saying. Nevertheless, as
unpopular as it may be in our contemporary cul-
ture, the fact is that the Christian life has very little
to do with personal happiness.

It is impossible to be happy in certain trials, but
God never promised us happiness. Bad stuff—evil

and horrifying stuff—simply happens. We may be
living or working in unfulfilling or miserable situations. We ought not put on fake happy faces and act
like nothing is wrong; that would be hypocrisy. We
can, however, experience joy and peace in the midst
of those situations. There is a vast difference
between happiness and joy. Happiness is a mood;
joy is a fruit of the Spirit (see Gal. 5:22–23). Joy is
a deep-seated assurance that comes through the
belief that, no matter what happens, God is ultimately in control. It is the conviction that He will
take the deepest, most hurtful things in our lives
and work them for our good. Romans 8:28 (KJV)
declares, "All things work together for good to
them that love God, to them who are the called
according to his purpose." That verse does not say
that all things are good or that God causes all
things, but that He will use all things—even terrible things—for our good. We will occasionally see
in this life the good that results from our trials.
More often, however, we will have to wait till we
get to heaven to recognize how God was working
in our painful situations.

CRACKED POTS

Above all, God delights in using cracked pots. In
2 Corinthians 4:7–9 (NKJV) the apostle Paul tells us,

"We have this treasure in earthen vessels, that the excellence of the power may be of God and not of us. We are hard-pressed on every side, yet not crushed; we are perplexed, but not in despair; persecuted, but not forsaken; struck down, but not destroyed." As Spirit-filled vessels of God, when we take the blows from life what's the result? We are not destroyed, and we are not crushed. But we do get cracked. And that is exactly what God wants to happen. You see, if we have the candle of God's Spirit lit inside our clay vessel, when we get cracked, His light shines out of us. The more cracks in our vessels, the more of God others can see in us.

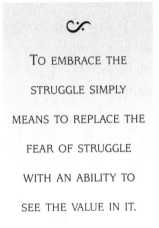

TO EMBRACE THE STRUGGLE SIMPLY MEANS TO REPLACE THE FEAR OF STRUGGLE WITH AN ABILITY TO SEE THE VALUE IN IT.

I've seen this time and again at funerals. At most funerals where the deceased was a Christ follower, there are often those in attendance who, after seeing the peace and hope being offered up, turn their lives over to the Lord. My uncle recently passed away, and I will miss him. But I was so moved by his life message and hope of eternity that the funeral actually motivated me to walk more closely with Christ.

Others in attendance were also moved to make serious changes in their lives.

When others see joy, peace, and love in the midst of our pain—and even our death—they find inspiration from the "hope that is in [us]" (1 Peter 3:15 KJV). Hurting people are rarely interested in our great exploits; they want to know the hope they see in us when we go through the same fires they are experiencing.

ADD SOME SPICE

A serious cook maintains a wide assortment of spices that have been dried, ground, and packaged. But if those spices remain on a stem, in the earth, or in a shell, their flavors and aromas stay locked away. It is the process of cracking, pounding, and breaking that releases the spices' flavors and aromas. Without the breaking, the pungent aromas and flavors can't be experienced.

A crack in our vessel can lead to hopelessness. It can also lead to healing and opportunity. It is through life's cracks that we become more compassionate, more understanding, and more in tune with the needs of others. Paul wrote in 2 Corinthians 1:3–4, "Praise be to the God and Father of our Lord Jesus Christ, the Father of compassion and the God of all comfort, who comforts us in all our troubles, so that we can comfort those in any trouble with the comfort we ourselves have received from God." If we let our brokenness release the inner aroma of God's Spirit, we, and those around us, can experience His healing.

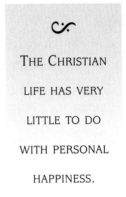

THE CHRISTIAN LIFE HAS VERY LITTLE TO DO WITH PERSONAL HAPPINESS.

When adversity strikes, we get cracked. If we allow God's light to shine through those cracks instead of trying to hide them, we become a mixture of reality and beauty. Imagine an old brown earthen pot sitting on a mantel. Covering its surface, zigzagging horizontally and vertically, are cracks. In the light of day, the pot looks common and worthless. But in the darkness, with a bright light inside, the ordinary pot is transformed into a dazzling array of brilliance. We see rays of light bursting out in all directions. But the pot shines the brightest when there is darkness surrounding it. Yousuf Karsh, a photographer most famous for his *Life* magazine photo of Winston Churchill, said, "Character, like a photograph, develops in darkness."[3] It's true.

Cracks make us real, and being real is what embracing the struggle is all about. The classic children's picture book *The Velveteen Rabbit* by

Margery Williams beautifully illustrates this truth. In the story two stuffed animals, the Skin Horse and the Velveteen Rabbit, engage in a conversation in the nursery.

> "What is REAL?" asked the Rabbit one day, when they were lying side by side near the nursery fender, before Nana came to tidy the room. "Does it mean having things that buzz inside you and a stick-out handle?"
> "Real isn't how you are made," said the Skin Horse. "It's a thing that happens to you. When a child loves you for a long, long time, not just to play with, but REALLY loves you, then you become Real."
> "Does it hurt?" asked the Rabbit.
> "Sometimes," said the Skin Horse, for he was always truthful. "When you are Real you don't mind being hurt."
> "Does it happen all at once, like being wound up," he asked. "Or bit by bit?"
> "It doesn't happen all at once, like being wound up," said the Skin Horse. "You become. It takes a long time.

HAPPINESS IS A MOOD; JOY IS A FRUIT OF THE SPIRIT.

That's why it doesn't often happen to people who break easily, or have sharp edges, or who have to be carefully kept. Generally, by the time you are Real, most of your hair has been loved off, and your eyes drop out and you get loose in the joints and very shabby. But these things don't matter at all, because once you are Real you can't be ugly, except to people who don't understand."[4]

Cracks in our vessels are blessings that come by means of our struggles. My son's deafness has come packaged with much pain, much struggle, and many cracks. Along with the pain, however, have also come many unexpected blessings. I'm developing a depth of character that could come in no way other than through this trial. I'm becoming a deeper person. James is becoming a deeper person. Pain and struggle will do that to people.

FROM THE HANDS OF CHILDREN

When James was about ten years old, I went by his school to observe. Recess was in progress, and I could see him on the playground playing with the other children. He was, at that time, being mainstreamed into a regular hearing school that also had a program for the deaf. For the first half of the day the ten or so deaf children met together, and for the second half of the day they were integrated with the hearing students. The recesses were combined. Off to the side was a little boy who was both deaf *and* blind. Teachers communicated with him by using sign language in his open hands. He would actually feel their hands as they signed. It was a remarkable sight to behold a means of communication that requires such patience from both the signer and signee.

My eyes moistened as I watched my son, the one with all that high energy, the "Wild Thing" as I had called him on numerous occasions, patiently and compassionately hand-signing to this deaf and blind child. It was precious as the boy tenderly felt James' hands, seeming surprised that someone other than a teacher was taking time with him. After James finished signing, he gently turned the boy in the direction he needed to go and walked with him to his desired destination. In the background, the sounds of children playing blended with that of balls bouncing and jump ropes smacking on concrete. Most of the hearing kids didn't even notice the boy. They were too busy playing. Others avoided him. Yet James, at ten years of age, understood this boy's frustration and took time, his highly valued recess time, to communicate with him.

James wasn't embarrassed or too busy. He wasn't worried about what his friends thought. He wasn't afraid to touch someone who was either different or unlovely. That's depth! That's maturity! And it has come because James himself has had to struggle. My temptation as a father is to try to remove struggles from his life. But I'm learning that God is using the struggles to mold James into the compassionate person he is today. As difficult as it may be to understand, trials, afflictions, and struggles have a way of instilling compassion and understanding in our hearts. Especially if in the midst of them we choose to trust God.

ALL THE BEAUTY OF THE UNIVERSE

I'm reminded of Helen Keller, someone whose life has been a source of great inspiration and hope for many.

Helen was born a normal, healthy child on June 27, 1880, on a small northwest Alabama cotton plantation. When she was nineteen months old, Helen fell ill with scarlet fever. For many days Helen was expected to die. When the fever finally broke, Helen's family was relieved that their daughter had survived. Helen's mother soon noticed, though, that her daughter failed to respond when the dinner bell rang or when she passed her hand in front of her daughter's eyes. Helen had survived her illness, but it had ruthlessly stolen her hearing and her sight. Helen Keller had become both deaf and blind.

The decade that followed proved extremely difficult for Helen and her family. Frustrated and confused, Helen became uncontrollable, smashing dishes and lamps and terrorizing the whole household with her temper tantrums. Relatives regarded her as a monster and insisted she be institutionalized. But the Kellers wouldn't hear of it. After much counsel and searching, they eventually employed a young woman named Anne Sullivan to work with Helen.

Anne herself had learned to thrive on the jagged edges of disability and loss. By the age of five she had lost the majority of her sight. By the time Anne was ten, her mother had died and her father deserted her. She and her brother, Jimmie, lived in an orphanage where he died in his teenage years, leaving her completely alone.

Although she was able to read print for short periods of time, Anne read Braille as well. She

> IT IS THROUGH LIFE'S CRACKS THAT WE BECOME MORE COMPASSIONATE, MORE UNDERSTANDING, AND MORE IN TUNE WITH THE NEEDS OF OTHERS.

attended the Perkins Institution for the Blind and planned to be a teacher, but due to her poor eyesight, finding work was nearly impossible. When she received the offer to serve as Helen's teacher, she accepted.

Anne immediately started teaching Helen to finger spell. Her first word was *doll* to signify a present she had bought to give to Helen. The next word she taught Helen was *cake*. Although Helen could repeat these finger movements, she could not understand what they meant. And while Anne was laboring to help her understand, she also struggled to keep Helen's behavior under control. Like a wild animal, Helen had become accustomed to climbing onto the dinner table and eating with her hands from the plates of everyone seated there.

CRACKS IN OUR VESSELS ARE BLESSINGS THAT COME BY MEANS OF OUR STRUGGLES.

To improve Helen's behavior, she and Anne moved into a small cottage near the main house. Anne's attempts to improve Helen's table manners, and make her brush her hair and button her shoes led to increasingly violent temper tantrums, which Anne addressed by refusing to finger spell on Helen's hands.

Over the weeks, Helen's behavior dramatically improved, and a bond between the two grew. Then, on April 5, 1887, a "miracle" breakthrough occurred. Up until that point, Helen had not fully understood the meaning of the words Anne would finger spell, but on that day, when Anne led her to the water pump, everything changed.

As Anne pumped the water over Helen's hand, she spelled out the word *water* into Helen's free hand. Something clicked in Helen's brain, and Anne could immediately see that she understood. Helen enthusiastically asked Anne for the name of the pump to be spelled on her hand and then the name of the trellis. All the way back to the house, Helen excitedly learned the names of everything she touched and also asked for Anne's name. Anne spelled the name *teacher* on Helen's hand. Within the next few hours, Helen learned the spelling of thirty new words.

From that point on, Helen's progress was astonishing. Her ability to learn was far beyond anything anyone had ever seen among the deaf and blind. Before long Anne was teaching Helen to read—first with raised letters and later with Braille—then to write with both standard and Braille typewriters.

Helen Keller went on to become the first deaf and blind person to enroll at an institution of higher learning. She graduated on June 28, 1904, from

Radcliffe College, becoming the first deaf and blind person to earn a Bachelor of Arts degree. Helen found fame as an author of many inspiring books, as a lecturer, and as a representative of the American Foundation for the Blind. Consider her words:

> As we trust God and embrace struggle instead of resisting it, we will grow and thrive.

Difficulties meet us at every turn. They are the accompaniment of life. They result from combinations of character and individual idiosyncrasies. The surest way to meet them is to assume that we are immortal and that we have a Friend who "slumbers not, nor sleeps," and who watches over us and guides us—if we but trust Him.

With this thought strongly entrenched in our inmost being, we can do almost anything we wish and need not limit the things we think. We may help ourselves to all the beauty of the universe that we can hold. For every hurt there is recompense of tender sympathy. Out of pain grow the violets of patience and

sweetness. The marvelous richness of
human experience would lose something
of rewarding joy if there were no limitations to overcome. The hilltop hour
would not be half so wonderful if there
were no dark valley to traverse.[5]

Helen Keller learned to thrive on the jagged
edge. She chose to trust God and refused to adopt a
victim mentality. As a result, her life has changed our
world.

If God could take care of Helen Keller in such a
magnificent way, surely He can take care of my son
James. He can also take care of you and me. As we
trust God and embrace struggle instead of resisting
it, we will grow and thrive.

TRUSTING GOD

*Meanwhile, where is God? ... When you are
happy, so happy that you have no sense of
needing Him, if you turn to Him then
with praise, you will be welcomed with open
arms. But go to Him when your need is
desperate, when all other help is vain and
what do you find? A door slammed in your
face and a sound of bolting and double
bolting on the inside. After that, silence.*

—C. S. LEWIS

Matthew 10:30 can't be any clearer: "And even
the very hairs of your head are all numbered." You've

never seen my son's hair, but I'll give you a clue what it's like. His e-mail address has the word *moppy* in it. If God actually has the hairs of his head numbered, He is a great God indeed! For the longest time, I regarded that verse as unrealistic, nothing more than a metaphor for God's omniscience. It was hard for me to believe that the actual hairs on my head were numbered. Does God really know the exact number of the hairs on everyone's head—everyone throughout history? Would He even care? What would be the point? That's what I used to think. Then over the past twenty years I've been researching and studying Christian apologetics, science, nature, the universe, and the human body. What I've found is that Jesus meant exactly what He said. Our hairs *are* numbered. It simply took science centuries to confirm what God already knew. Multiple times in the Bible God presents scientific truth that predates the scientific method. The following summaries are but a few

> ℘
>
> THE ONE WHO HAS
> DESIGNED THE
> UNIVERSE AND ALL
> LIFE IS THE GOD OF
> THE UNIVERSE. IN
> ORDER TO THRIVE
> ON THE JAGGED EDGE
> WE MUST KNOW
> THAT GOD IS AND
> ACKNOWLEDGE THAT
> HE IS IN CONTROL.

examples cited in Grant R. Jeffrey's book *The Signature of God*.

GENESIS 2:7

"And the LORD God formed man of the dust of the ground" (KJV). For years scientists scoffed at the simplicity of God's using basic clay to form the human body. However, after decades of systematic assessments and examinations of the essentials that make up the human body, scientists have been startled to find that ordinary soil contains every single element found in the human body.

LEVITICUS 17:11

"For the life of the flesh is in the blood" (KJV). This statement revealed advanced scientific knowledge at a time when the level of pagan medical knowledge was abysmal. Now, of course, we know our blood is essential to many of our body's life processes. The blood carries nutrients and materials that produce growth and

healing, store energy as fat, and support
every organ in our body. When the blood
supply is restricted to any part of the
body, that part immediately begins to
die. Blood is essential to fighting disease,
clotting wounds, and growing new skin
and cells. For centuries ignorant doctors
"bled" their patients by draining large
amounts of blood from their bodies in a
vain attempt to defeat disease. They did
not realize that our blood is the key to
our flesh. Truly, as the Bible declares,
"the life of the flesh is in the blood."

JOB 28:24–26

"For he looketh to the ends of the earth,
and seeth under the whole heaven; to
make the weight for the winds; and he
weigheth the waters by measure. When
he made a decree for the rain, and a way
for the lightning of the thunder" (KJV).
In this intriguing statement the Bible
reveals that the winds are governed by
their weight, a fact that scientists have
only determined in the last century.
How could Job have known that the air

and the wind patterns are governed by
their actual weight? Meteorologists have
found that the relative weights of the
wind and water greatly determine the
weather patterns.[1]

I could go on. Volumes have been written on the
subject. It's all there in black and white. But now I
want to get back to the number of hairs on our
heads.

How Many Hairs?

Does God really know the actual number of the individual hairs on our heads? The answer lies in our
DNA. Each strand of DNA located within each individual cell contains a highly detailed genetic code that
determines everything from the color of our eyes to
the length of our toes to our talents and tendencies.
Your DNA is like a complex program, which, if we
were to load it onto a computer, would produce an
elaborate design along with a detailed plan for your
assembly! Each single strand of DNA contains so
much information that scientists who study genetics
realize that the information encoded in an individual's
DNA contains data equivalent to a thousand encyclo-
pedias. The sheer volume of information is staggering
and points clearly to a Designer who is infinitely more

intelligent than any Nobel Prize–winning scientist. Read what Dr. Stephen C. Meyer, who earned his PhD from Cambridge University, said about DNA.

> While many [scientists] outside origin-of-life [fields] may still invoke "chance" as a causal explanation for the origin of biological information, few serious researchers still do.... Chance is not an adequate explanation for the origin of biological complexity and specificity.... Our experience with information-intensive systems indicates that such systems always come from an intelligent source—i.e., from mental or personal agents, not chance.... During the last forty years, every naturalistic model proposed has failed to explain the origin of information.... Thus, mind or intelligence or what philosophers call "agent causation" [intelligent designer], now stands as the only cause known to be capable of creating an information-rich system, including the coding regions of DNA.[2]

Richard Swenson, MD, in his book *More Than Meets the Eye*, elaborated on Meyer's comments:

If we observe design, it is not wrong to infer a Designer. If we observe life, it is not wrong to infer a Life-giver. If we see DNA, it is not wrong to infer the precision of a Genius.... Everywhere we see life—from simple to highly developed forms—we see order. This order involves coded information in the form of DNA. Any serious thinker is confronted with two unavoidable questions: How did non-life first step across the threshold to become life? And how did life encode immensely complex amounts of information on DNA? Time plus chance has no answers for these questions. Randomness is not a solution. If we see information and intelligence and intention, it is not wrong to infer that "behind the dim unknown, standeth God within the shadow, keeping watch above his own."[3]

GOD KNOWS EVERYTHING ABOUT US EVEN THOUGH OUR CIRCUMSTANCES MAY SEEM TO INDICATE OTHERWISE, ESPECIALLY WHEN GOD APPEARS TO BE SILENT AND DISTANT.

The One who has designed the universe and all life is the God of the universe. In order to thrive on the jagged edge we must know that God is and acknowledge that He is in control. Hebrews 11:6 says, "Anyone who comes to him must believe that he exists." The God who created DNA even encoded our DNA with the number of hairs each of us has on our head. Each hair contains our DNA. In fact, in some criminal cases, it's the DNA pulled from a single hair that has convicted or freed a person.

THE SILENT DESIGNER

Yes, we were created by the Great Designer. And where there is design, there is also purpose. God knows everything about us even though our circumstances may seem to indicate otherwise, especially when God appears to be silent and distant. That's a problem, isn't it? Sure, Romans 1:20 (KJV) says, "The invisible things of him from the creation of the world are clearly seen, being understood by the things that are made, even his eternal power and Godhead." But God often seems silent.

My sister is an audiologist. A few years ago she ran a hearing test on an eighteen-year-old man who had been deaf since infancy. He told her, "I've been praying for years that I would be able to hear. Now I think I'm hearing some sounds." His faith and hopes were high.

He was sure the tests would reveal that his hearing was improving. But the tests revealed no change. The man was just as deaf as he had ever been. When my sister broke the news to him, tears of disappointment ran down his cheeks. My sister, too, was heartbroken. The young man's mother said to my sister, "Don't worry about him. He'll be fine. He's used to this."

Can you imagine getting used to this type of disappointment? I'm sure that, more than once, this young man has asked, "Where are You, God? Why have You abandoned me? Have You not heard my prayers?" He, too, felt the cold silence that C. S. Lewis described in the quote at the start of this chapter.

In the novel *Clover* by Doris Sanders, the book's main character, a ten-year-old girl named Clover, has to deal with the sudden death of her father in an automobile crash. And this after her mother had died a few years earlier. I think Clover captures how many of us sometimes feel about God's silence.

> My aunt wanted to pray for me. With me.
> I didn't feel like praying. It seemed like all
> the praying I'd done hadn't helped any-
> way, not one single bit. While I was hiding
> behind those trays [in the hospital nurses'
> station], I prayed for my daddy not to die.
> I'd prayed for my grandpa, too. Even
> prayed for my mama to come back to me.

I just can't pray no more. It won't do me
any good no way.[4]

BIBLE BASEBALL

James loves sports, and he's a good athlete. Because
of his deafness, however, he requires extra attention.
Most coaches have no idea how to communicate with
the deaf; neither do they have the time to focus on
one player. As a result, James has had to learn mostly
by his observation of other players.

One summer I volunteered to coach a Little
League baseball team at the YMCA. I figured that
because I knew sign language, I could sign to James
and talk to the hearing kids at the same time. It would
be no big deal. When I registered my son, I made a
point not to tell anyone James was deaf. It was important to me that he receive no special treatment and
that he get an equal chance. When the first coaches'
meeting came around, I again mentioned nothing
about my son's deafness.

Baton Rouge, where we live, is a relatively large
city. I didn't know any of the other coaches, and they
didn't know me. At the meeting, we were given our
team rosters and told to contact the players' parents
before a certain date and set up practice. After the
meeting, I went home. That was it.

A few days after the coaches' meeting, I received a phone call from the YMCA's director. The call went something like this:

Bill: Mr. Davis, this is Bill at the YMCA. I was wondering if you could help us with a little problem. We have two deaf boys who are looking for a team to get on. Would you be willing to allow them on your team?

GOD KNOWS WHAT'S GOING ON, AND HIS PLAN IS BIGGER THAN OURS.

Max: How did you find out that my son is deaf and that I know sign language?

Bill: I didn't.

Max: Wait a minute. You had no idea I have a deaf son and that I know sign?

Bill: That's correct.

Max: Then why did you call me?

Bill: I just picked your name from our coaches' list.

Max: Of course I'll take them! This means we have three deaf kids on our team. James will be thrilled!

The story gets even better. Later that week, I started calling the parents of the children on my roster.

When I got to boy number thirteen, his mother warned me in a concerned fashion, "Now I want you to understand that Aaron is deaf and will require some special help." I just about leaped out of my chair! We had ten teams in the YMCA that year. Out of all ten teams, how many deaf kids do you think there were? You got it. Only four, and *all four* ended up on my team! For me, it was a sign from God. He was meeting the needs of four deaf kids with a coach who knew sign language and friends they could bond with. I coached those boys for several years, and to this day they remain friends.

The message comes screaming back to me: Even though I don't understand *why* James is deaf, and I desperately want him to hear, something bigger is going on. It dwarfs my limited understanding. God knows *exactly* where James is, and He cares for James as much as I do. God took something as ordinary as baseball to demonstrate this to me. Peace enters my heart when I recognize His care for my son.

There is another astonishing story I must relate. It happened in, of all places, the steam room and whirlpool at my local health club.

MATT'S DREAM

John (not his real name) is a leviathan of a man who could intimidate the strongest of us. Yet, he has a quiet and gentle spirit and loves God dearly. I've worked out alongside him at the health club for more than ten years. At this writing, it's been a year since his teenage son Matt (not his real name) was abducted. Like all abductions, it was the top story on the broadcast news. Volunteers hung posters and conducted searches. To date, the boy has not been found, and the authorities have concluded that Matt is most likely dead. Matt was an outspoken Christian and a model student. He was not involved in any questionable activities. Everybody loved him. He was one of those kids who lit up a room when he entered it. His disappearance shocked everyone who knew him.

I had given John a copy of my last book, *Desperate Dependence*, and soon after that I ran into him in the steam room. John said his wife had snatched the book from him and couldn't put it down, but that he was going to read it as soon as she was finished.

> WE'RE TO TRUST GOD, NOT WITH OUR MINDS OR EMOTIONS ONLY, BUT WITH ALL OUR HEARTS.

John told me he liked to come in the steam room to pray and prepare mentally before he went home to be with his wife and other children. He felt the pressure of having to hold up the rest of the family emotionally and spiritually. For the next few minutes, he opened his pain to me.

I then shared with him a story about a Baptist preacher named Don Piper who was involved in a head-on car collision and was pronounced dead. Don's spirit left his body, and he found himself in God's presence. His story is amazing. You can read it in his book, *90 Minutes in Heaven.*[5]

As I was relating this story to John, his eyes filled with tears, and he seemed somewhat startled. I thought at first I might have offended him. Then he said, "I'm going to tell you something I've never told anyone outside my immediate family. I've never told anyone because I don't want people to think I'm out of my mind." John went on to tell me that a week or so before Matt was abducted, his son entered their bedroom, took his mother by the hand (John had left for work), and in a very serious manner shared an unusual experience he had had the night before while lying on his bed. Matt said that his spirit had left his body, and he had found himself in God's presence. He described the event as more vivid than any dream he had ever had. Matt went on to tell his mother about the wonders of heaven, about seeing certain people who had died, and about seeing angels. After Matt had spent some time on the other side, he was told he had to return. He was disappointed because he didn't want to leave the warmth and peace that enveloped him. When Matt asked why he had to go back, the angel escorting him replied, "Your mother and father are not ready yet."

Matt's experience seems to compare somewhat with the apostle Paul's vision: "I know a man in Christ who fourteen years ago was caught up to the third heaven. Whether it was in the body or out of the body I do not know—God knows. And I know that this man—whether in the body or apart from the body I do not know, but God knows—was caught up to paradise" (2 Cor. 12:2–4).

Why would God allow a boy to have a vision of heaven, send him back to earth with a specific message— "Your mother and father are not ready yet"—and then still allow him to be abducted? God obviously knew ahead of time what was going to happen and that at some point in the future the parents would be ready. It just doesn't make sense to the natural mind. But the message of Matt's story is that God knows what's going on, and His plan is bigger than ours. For me, the question remains: Why would God do something that proves He knows exactly where my son James is, but still allow him to struggle with deafness? I don't know. It's at such times that we must turn to simple but not simplistic verses such as "Trust in the LORD with all your heart and lean not on your own understanding" (Prov. 3:5). We've known that verse

since we were children, but when we really take it
seriously, it's difficult to apply. It implies that we'll
be facing circumstances and events that we won't
understand. At those times, we're to trust God, not
with our minds or emotions only, but with all our
hearts.

There is a time when we must let go of our own
understanding and cling to the conviction that God
knows more than we do about how to run this universe. When we trust Him, we will come to the same
conclusion that Job did.

KNOW GOD, KNOW PEACE

After Job offered up all his questions, complaints, and
pain up to God, God finally answered. Yet He didn't
answer *all* Job's questions. God simply responded,

> Where were you when I laid the earth's
> foundation? Tell me, if you understand.
> Who marked off its dimensions? Surely
> you know! Who stretched a measuring
> line across it? ... Can you bind the beauti-
> ful Pleiades? Can you loose the cords of
> Orion? ... Do you know the laws of the
> heavens? Can you set up God's dominion
> over the earth? ... Does the hawk take
> flight by your wisdom and spread his

wings toward the south? Does the eagle
soar at your command? (Job 38:4–5, 31,
33; 39:26–27)

After God's reply, Job concluded, "Surely I spoke
of things I did not understand, things too wonderful
for me to know.... Therefore I ... repent in dust and
ashes" (42:3, 6). Job realized that God was bigger
and wiser, and he chose to put his trust in those real-
ities. Regardless of the tragedies that had befallen
him, Job was able to say, "I know that my Redeemer
lives.... Yet will I hope in him" (19:25; 13:15). Job
could say this, not because he knew why God allowed
his trials, but because he knew God!

The same held true for the apostle Paul. Paul's
confidence in God, even as he endured his thorn in
the flesh and other hardships, was not based on his
knowledge of why those things happened. Rather, his
confidence rested on his knowledge of God Himself.
Paul wrote in 2 Timothy 1:12, "I know whom I have
believed." The God he trusted was the One who, by
His power, had set the universe into motion and who,
in His infinite wisdom, had numbered the very hairs
on his head. But for Paul, the ultimate expression of
God's awesome character was demonstrated when He
laid aside His divinity, becoming a servant, and dying
for us: "He who did not spare his own Son, but gave
him up for us all—how will he not also, along with

him, graciously give us all things?" (Rom. 8:32). When God became one of us and took on our pain, He not only identified with us, He also proved His intention: "For we have not an high priest which cannot be touched with the feeling of our infirmities" (Heb. 4:15 KJV). It's important to know that God feels our pain. The feelings of our infirmities have touched Him.

Joni Eareckson Tada, a long-term quadriplegic, put it this way: "When He covers our eyes with the blanket of a limited understanding, surely He deserves to be given 'the benefit of the doubt,' to put it mildly. He is worthy of our trust."[6]

And this is not some irrational blind trust, but a solid faith based on reason, solid science, that comes to life in relationship with Him. Even so, 1 Corinthians 13:12 declares, "Now we see but a poor reflection as in a mirror.... Now I know in part; then I shall know fully."

One who thrives is one who trusts in God's sovereignty even when he may not understand the whys or have the answers to God's apparent silence in those moments when we desperately long to hear His voice.

WHEN FEAR WHISPERS

Fear whispers to us that God is not really big enough to take care of us. It tells us we are not really safe in his hands. It causes us to distort the way we think about him.

—JOHN ORTBERG

Awoman once said to me in a half-joking manner prompted by anger and pain, "Sure, I can trust God … I can trust Him to push me off a cliff!" After committing her life to Christ at an early age and serving Him for years, she had experienced a long series of disappointments and heartaches. Life had not turned out the way she had planned. Although she loved God and believed He was real, she had become cynical about trusting God to accomplish positive results without extreme pain. Fear whispered to her, "If you really trust God, if you commit everything to Him, He'll let you fall flat on your face."

God may have given you a dream for your life. You want so badly for it to be fulfilled, but fear whispers in your ear, "God really doesn't know best. If you give up control, if you stop manipulating the situation and put it completely into God's hands, the dream won't happen."

> WHEN FEAR HAUNTS US, IT PARALYZES US, CHAINS US, AND RENDERS US UNABLE TO MOVE FORWARD WITH THE LIFE GOD DESIRES FOR US.

A gifted Bible teacher once told me, "One way to tell if you're in God's will is to realize that if He doesn't come through, you'll be dead meat!" Sometimes, when we find ourselves in those situations, fear whispers, "If you wholeheartedly turn it over to God, He will surely let you become dead meat." Stan Toler wrote a best-selling book with the zany title, *God Has Never Failed Me, but He's Sure Scared Me to Death a Few Times.*[1] Most of us can relate! We often seem to hear the voice of fear whispering in our ears, "If you really trust God, if you truly depend on Him, He may come through, but before He does, He's going to take you to the edge and scare you to death!"

CHAINS OF FEAR

One of the side effects of life's trials is fear—the fear of failure, the fear of pain, the fear that God is not going to come through for us, the fear that God is going to let something terrible happen to us: *What if I ask God for money to pay my bills and, instead, I lose my income? What if I pray for God's protection over my loved ones and tragedy strikes? What if, instead of comfort, I receive sorrow? What if, instead of security, I'm thrust into the depths of uncertainty?*

Fear is a real and ever-present force that comes to us in myriad packages. One thing is certain though: When fear haunts us, it paralyzes us, chains us, and renders us unable to move forward with the life God desires for us. But that is not God's plan. He wants us to be free of the chains of fear and to experience the peace and rest that come from trusting Him. If we are to thrive on the jagged edge, we must deal with our fears. Isaiah 35:4 declares, "Say to those with fearful hearts, 'Be strong, do not fear; your God will come.'" Second Timothy 1:7 (KJV) says,

"For God hath not given us the spirit of fear; but of power, and of love, and of a sound mind." John 14:27 (NASB) says, "Peace I leave with you; My peace I give to you; not as the world gives do I give to you. Do not let your heart be troubled, nor let it be fearful."

Did you know that the Bible exhorts us at least 366 times not to fear? That single command occurs more frequently than any other. Why is that? Why is fear so unhealthy? The following are just a few reasons.

FOUR REASONS FEAR IS UNHEALTHY

1. Fear Frustrates Faith and Hinders Trust in and Obedience to God

Hebrews 11:6 says, "Without faith it is impossible to please God." We cannot please God without faith, and it's impossible to act in faith when fear controls us. It obstructs faith. Fear and faith are in conflict—one is positive, the other negative. Harry Emerson Fosdick said it well: "Fear imprisons, faith liberates; fear paralyzes, faith empowers; fear disheartens, faith encourages; fear sickens, faith heals; fear makes useless, faith makes serviceable—and, most of all, fear puts hopelessness at the heart of life, while faith rejoices in God."[2]

2. Fear Delays Our Destiny

God has blessed each of us with certain gifts and abilities that He desires for us to develop and use. But when fear paralyzes us, our gifts often stay buried and embryonic.

The Israelites wandered in the desert for forty years. An entire generation died without fulfilling their destiny because they were afraid of giants in the Promised Land and refused to go in and claim what God had given them. When we live in fear, we never experience the personal promised land to which God has called us. Psychiatrist Paul Tournier wrote, "All of us have reservoirs of full potential ... but the road that leads to those reservoirs is guarded by the dragon of fear."[3] Fear restrains us from serving others and thwarts our effectiveness in serving God. It immobilizes us, particularly when God is leading us to risk stepping out of our comfort zone.

3. Fear Damages Relationships

John Steinbeck wrote, "A person afraid is a dangerous animal."[4] Robert Frost put it this way: "The people I am most afraid of are the people who are scared."[5] Fear causes us to hurt both ourselves and others in senseless and damaging ways. When fear and insecurity occupy a relationship, it begins to sour. Trust falls apart. Fear keeps people trapped in

self-defeating patterns, hurting them and those
around them. It triggers overprotection and exces-
sive control. If we fear rejection, we tend to put on
facades, hide our true selves, and avoid authentic
communication, sabotaging relationships with those
important to us.

4. Fear Saps Our Strength

Nehemiah told his fellow Israelites, "The joy of the
LORD is your strength" (Neh. 8:10). I don't know
about you, but when my mind is filled with fearful
thoughts, I'm not very joyful. In fact, I'm just the
opposite. If I allow those negative and destructive
thoughts to remain, it will not be long before I'm in
a full-blown depression. Have you ever noticed that
it's difficult to be joyful and anxious at the same
time? Remember in chapter 2 we talked about joy
being deep-seated peace, assurance, and calm confidence that, no matter what happens, God is in
control. Confidence and strength come when we
have joy. Walking in fear saps that joy and robs us of
our strength.

Yes, fear is destructive in many ways. It is from
the Enemy, who desires to "steal and kill and
destroy" (John 10:10), and one of his primary tools
is fear. God wants to replace our fear with a courageous faith that gives us comforting peace in any
situation.

There are four biblical action steps that will help us conquer our fear so that we can thrive instead of merely survive.

FOUR STEPS TO FEARLESS FAITH AND COMFORTING PEACE

1. Develop a Healthy Fear

Healthy fear is not an oxymoron, but a tool fashioned by God for our protection. The absence of it would create a deficiency in our personalities, causing a shortage of common sense that would result in physical and emotional harm. Webster's dictionary defines *fear* as "an unpleasant emotional state characterized by anticipation of pain or danger."[6] Healthy fear keeps us from doing hazardous and senseless things.

> IF WE ARE TO THRIVE ON THE JAGGED EDGE, WE MUST DEAL WITH OUR FEARS.

A nineteen-year-old and two of his friends were killed a few years ago in an automobile accident near my home. He was driving his car so fast that he lost control and hit a tree head-on. The police confirmed that he was traveling well over one hundred miles per hour on a curvy, two-lane road. Most of the people who knew this young man also knew he had an "attitude." When the local news interviewed his girlfriend, she said she had ridden with him more than once at such high speeds. He was hotheaded. He was arrogant. He had a sticker on his car that read in big bold letters "NO FEAR." Now he's dead. His epitaph could have read, "NO FEAR. NO RESPECT. NOW DEAD." It's a tragic story. This young man could have used a dose of healthy fear. God wants us to use our brains and to experience healthy fear.

> We cannot please God without faith, and it's impossible to act in faith when fear controls us.

The Bible commands us to fear God. Proverbs 3:7 (NKJV) says, "Fear the LORD and depart from evil," and Proverbs 19:23 (KJV) tells us that "the fear of the LORD tendeth to life."

There are hundreds of other passages that urge us to fear the Lord. Proverbs 1:7 says, "The fear of the LORD is the beginning of knowledge." A healthy fear of God is the first step toward defeating the unhealthy fears that frustrate our faith. But hear me correctly; we are not talking about a mere optimistic respect, but an actual terror. "Knowing therefore the *terror* of the Lord, we persuade men" (2 Cor. 5:11 KJV). The

Greek word translated *terror* in this passage is *pho-
bos*, which means to be "exceedingly afraid."[7] I like
what Mark Tabb wrote in his book *Out of the
Whirlwind*: "To fear the Lord means more than
respect or obedience. Fear means fear, knee knocking, tongue sticking to the roof of the mouth, palm
sweating fear, the same fear that gripped Job. And
this fear is the beginning of wisdom."[8]

When the children of Israel heard God's voice
thunder from Mount Sinai, they were terrified and
begged Moses to keep God away from them. Isaiah
saw the Lord in a vision and fell on his face as
though dead. When Jesus quieted the gale while sail-
ing across the Sea of Galilee with His disciples, they
knelt before Him, stunned, trembling with fear.
When the angel of the Lord appeared to them, the
Roman soldiers who were guarding Christ's tomb
"shook for fear of him and became like dead men"
(Matt. 28:4 NASB). John on the Isle of Patmos saw
the Lord in His resurrected power and also fell down
before Him as though dead. Read John's description
of the risen Lord:

> His head and hair were white like wool,
> as white as snow, and his eyes were like
> blazing fire. His feet were like bronze
> glowing in a furnace, and his voice was
> like the sound of rushing waters.... and

out of his mouth came a sharp double-edged sword. His face was like the sun shining in all its brilliance.... I saw heaven standing open and there before me was a white horse, whose rider is called Faithful and True. With justice he judges and makes war. His eyes are like blazing fire, and on his head are many crowns. He has a name written on him that no one knows but he himself. He is dressed in a robe dipped in blood, and his name is the Word of God.... Out of his mouth comes a sharp sword with which to strike down the nations. "He will rule them with an iron scepter." He treads the winepress of the fury of the wrath of God Almighty. (Revelation 1:14–16; 19:11–13, 15)

> GOD WANTS TO REPLACE OUR FEARS WITH A COURAGEOUS FAITH THAT GIVES US COMFORTING PEACE IN ANY SITUATION.

When we have healthy fear of God, we see Him for who He is in all His greatness and glory. This view encourages humility and the understanding of our position before a Holy God. The beginning of the book of Job declares that Job "was blameless and upright; he feared God and shunned evil" (1:1). At the end of the book, after Job had aired all his questions to God, God exonerated him by declaring him to be in the right (see 42:8). Yet, when Job had a revelation of who God really is, he cried out to Him: "My ears had heard of you but now my eyes have seen you. Therefore I despise myself and repent in dust and ashes" (42:5–6).

My question is, if Job was so righteous, why did he need to repent? Why did he despise himself? Job repented because he suddenly saw himself in comparison to God in all His glory and greatness. To other humans Job may have been righteous, but when measured against God, he was a mere mortal, full of sin, unbelief, and ignorance of eternal truths bigger than himself. He had a healthy fear. Healthy fear not only helps us see God for who He really is; it opens our eyes to our true selves as well.

Oswald Chambers wrote, "The remarkable thing about fearing God is that when you fear God you fear nothing else, whereas if you do not fear God you fear everything else."9 When we have a healthy fear of God, it's because we, like Job, have seen and understood His greatness. Fixing our eyes on God in this way is critical to overcoming unhealthy fears.

Whereas the first step toward a fearless faith has to do with fear, the second has to do with truth.

2. Apply God's Truth to Feelings and Circumstances

King David understood the need to apply God's truth to his emotions and the events he faced, and he expressed it in his writings. Regardless of how much he hurt or how intense his situation, he always turned his eyes to the God who was bigger than his circumstances and then declared the truth of who He is. David dealt with enemies, wayward children, loneliness, isolation, betrayal, sickness, and the consequences of his own sin and failure. It was while in the clutches of his deepest despair that David wrote:

HEALTHY FEAR IS NOT AN OXY-MORON, BUT A TOOL FASH-IONED BY GOD FOR OUR PROTECTION.

Be merciful to me, O LORD, for I am in distress; my eyes grow weak with sorrow, my soul and my body with grief. My life is consumed by anguish and my years by groaning; my strength fails because of my affliction, and my bones grow weak.
Because of all my enemies, I am the utter contempt of my neighbors; I am a dread

to my friends—those who see me on the
street flee from me. I am forgotten by
them as though I were dead; I have
become like broken pottery. For I hear
the slander of many; there is terror on
every side; they conspire against me and
plot to take my life. (Psalm 31:9–13)

Yes, David knew pain and suffering. Yet even in
his agony he chose to focus on the truth of God's
faithfulness. Read the very next verse. "But I trust in
you, O LORD; I say, 'You are my God'" (v. 14). What
powerful words! David readily acknowledged his
pain. Fear had surely whispered in his ear that all was
lost, that he was doomed. David nevertheless chose
by an act of his will to interrupt his flow of despair
with the little word *but*. His sorrows were great,
"But," he seemed to be saying, "I have seen God's
greatness.... But, I know who He really is.... But, I
place my trust in the God who I know loves me, who
cannot lie, who is faithful, who promised He would
sustain me." David continued his praise to God in
verses 19 and 24: "How great is your goodness,
which you have stored up for those who fear you ...
on those who take refuge in you.... Be strong and
take heart, all you who hope in the LORD." David
never lost his vision of the truth of God's greatness
and character. That's why the psalms are sprinkled

not only with honest assessments of his anguish, but also declarations of God's greatness and faithfulness: "The LORD is my light and my salvation; whom shall I fear? The LORD is the strength of my life; of whom shall I be afraid?" (27:1 NKJV).

When we focus on God's faithfulness, we gain His perspective. Our fears begin to dissolve, and His peace replaces them. It doesn't mean that we're exempt from difficulties or pain. But we begin to know and believe that we can trust Him in the midst of our circumstances, for He is trustworthy.

Romans 10:17 (KJV) tells us where faith comes from: "So then faith cometh by hearing, and hearing by the word of God." When fear attacks us, we must attack fear with the truth of God's Word. It's imperative that we "demolish arguments and every pretension that sets itself up against the knowledge of God, and [that] we take captive every thought to make it obedient to Christ" (2 Cor. 10:5). When under an onslaught of fears, we must also

> put on the full armor of God, so that
> when the day of evil comes, [we] may be
> able to stand [our] ground, and after
> [we] have done everything, to stand. [We
> must] stand firm then, with the belt of
> truth buckled around [our] waist, with
> the breastplate of righteousness in place,

and with [our] feet fitted with the readi-
ness that comes from the gospel of peace.
In addition to all this, [we must] take up
the shield of faith, with which [we] can
extinguish all the flaming arrows of the
evil one. [We must] take the helmet of
salvation and the sword of
the Spirit, which is the word
of God. And [we must] pray
in the Spirit. (Ephesians
6:13–18)

A walk of fearless faith and comforting peace requires us to focus,
not on our feelings, but on the
truth. Consider Ted. All through
high school and college, Ted never
had a date. He didn't go to the
prom. He was nice looking and
intelligent, but he continually bat-
tled with low self-esteem. He liked
women but never could get the
courage to ask anyone out. Because
he was such an introvert, he never
allowed himself to be in a position
even to meet women. Ted was over thirty-five years
old before he finally got the courage to ask someone
out. Whenever his friends and family addressed the

ℭℯ

A HEALTHY

FEAR OF GOD

IS THE FIRST

STEP TOWARD

DEFEATING

THE

UNHEALTHY

FEARS THAT

FRUSTRATE

OUR FAITH.

issue with Ted, he would just say he had a hard time meeting new people.

The truth was that Ted suffered from a deep fear of rejection. But his fear of rejection was only a surface diagnosis. The root cause of his fear went all the way back to his early childhood. When Ted was only five years old, his dad and mom divorced. His mom left his dad because his dad was an alcoholic and was physically and verbally abusive. Ted's mother remarried, and he was raised by his stepfather. But deep wounds remained embedded in his heart.

As he grew, Ted never dealt with his emotional pain. To survive, he simply pushed his pain deeper and deeper into his subconscious. All through childhood and adolescence, Ted felt he never quite fit in with the rest of the family. He never saw his biological dad again, and his mother and stepfather had two children of their own, which left Ted feeling even more like an outcast.

WE CAN PROLONG OUR PAIN AND SUFFERING BY DISOBEDIENCE AND DISTRUST, BY INDULGING OUR EMOTIONS RATHER THAN TAKING OUR THOUGHTS CAPTIVE TO THE TRUTH OF GOD'S WORD.

For thirty-six years Ted carried this emotional baggage; but because it had been buried for so long, the fears and insecurities simply became a part of his personality. Ted eventually married. His unresolved fears and insecurities are now negatively affecting his marriage. For himself and for his family, Ted needs to get a grip on his fears. The only way he will be free from the chains that bind him is to apply truth to the lies he's believed about himself. It won't be easy, but it is the only way.

The apostle John proclaimed that Jesus said, "You will know the truth, and the truth will set you free" (John 8:32). Remember, fear binds and truth frees. Once we understand the truth about ourselves, our situations, and our God, we can sever our unhealthy fears and stop believing lies. Truth frees people. Sadly, it is often difficult to accept the truth when we have believed a lie for so long.

Ted has been carrying false guilt and shame for most of his life. He believed, due to the abusive actions of his father, that he was not worthy of true love and acceptance from other people, and especially from God. His father had burdened him with unwarranted shame and guilt and had told him numerous lies, such as "You're not worth anything" and "You're stupid." Ted needed to see that God demonstrated his worth by sending Jesus to die for him.

This same truth applies to you and me and transcends what people do or say to us. It is a higher law. Romans 8:33 (NLT) declares, "Who dares accuse us whom God has chosen for his own? Will God? No! He is the one who has given us right standing with himself". Ted's earthly father may have said, "I wish you were never born!" But God says, "Before I formed you in the womb I knew you, before you were born I set you apart; I appointed you as a prophet to the nations" (Jer. 1:5).

It's important to note that we can prolong our pain and suffering by disobedience and distrust, by indulging our emotions rather than taking our thoughts captive to the truth of God's Word.

Like King David, Ted can experience fearless faith and comforting peace when he sees the truth of God's Word and applies it to his particular circumstance. So can you!

The third step toward a fearless faith requires love, but not just any kind of love. It is a love that is perfect.

3. Remember That Perfect Love Defeats Fear

"There is no fear in love. But perfect love drives out fear, because fear has to do with punishment. The one who fears is not made perfect in love" (1 John 4:18).

Sometimes we get confused when we try to reconcile God's telling us hundreds of times in the Bible to fear Him with the message of 1 John 4:18, which says, "There is no fear in love." It seems that if we fear God, then it's impossible to love Him. But that can't be right. While we could break down the preceding verse and devote an entire chapter to it, let's focus primarily on the perfect love of God that drives out fear.

It's easy to get the impression that the God of the Old Testament was once angry, harsh, and unforgiving. Then Jesus came along, and God somehow changed into the loving, merciful, gentle, and forgiving Father we now worship. But that is not at all the case. It was God who from the beginning initiated the whole plan of redemption. It was God who sent His Son to show us that He *is* perfect love. John 1:1, 14 says, "In the beginning was the Word, and the Word was with God, and the Word was God.... The Word became flesh and made his dwelling among us."

It is vital to maintain a healthy fear of God in the sense of recognizing His greatness and standing in awe of His glory, majesty, and power. But when we enter a personal relationship with Him via the cross,

> A HEALTHY FEAR OF GOD BECKONS US TO BE HUMBLE, TO RECOGNIZE HIS PROVISION, AND TO FEAR NOTHING BUT UNBELIEF.

and we understand His love for us, we need no longer fear His wrath. Paul wrote, "Consider therefore the kindness and sternness of God: sternness to those who fell, but kindness to you, provided that you continue in his kindness" (Rom. 11:22). God loves us perfectly, and by that love He made a way for us through the cross. Now, all He asks is that we continue in His kindness by faith and trust, not fearing His wrath. The only thing that can come between us and God is our unbelief. A healthy fear of God beckons us to be humble, to recognize His provision, and to fear nothing but unbelief.

> TAKING ACTION, OF COURSE, SOMETIMES MEANS WAITING ON GOD FOR HIS DIRECTION.

After His resurrection, Christ sent His Holy Spirit to reside in us and to impart to us that same power to deal with our own fears. That's why the apostle Paul wrote that "God hath not given us the spirit of fear; but of power, and of love, and of a sound mind" (2 Tim. 1:7 KJV).

Fear comes from the enemy; God replaces that spirit of fear with His Spirit, who gives us power to stand firm. By that same Spirit He imparts the love to extend His compassion for others, as well as a sound mind for clear reasoning. We don't have to walk in the spirit of fear, and we don't have to be afraid of the Father.

But there is a fourth step we must take if we are to have fearless faith.

4. Take Action Now

The fourth and final step to fearless faith and comforting peace is to take action. Just as fear paralyzes faith, action paralyzes fear. Something supernatural happens when we take even one single step forward. Faith happens. And when faith happens, miracles take place. John Ortberg wrote, "One small step of action is often worth a hundred internal pep talks.... God made us in such a way that taking one single step of action can be extremely powerful in robbing failure of its power."[10]

Taking action, of course, sometimes means waiting on God for His direction. Then, when He gives it, we must step out in obedience.

"Once you have come to believe God," wrote Henry Blackaby, "you demonstrate your faith by what you do.... action is required."[11] Many times, God will ask us to take that first action step of faith at the very point of our fears—mainly because He wants us to rise above them.

In his wonderful book *If You Want to Walk on Water You've Got to Get Out of the Boat*, to which I've referred several times, John Ortberg used the climax of the movie *Indiana Jones and the Last Crusade* to illustrate the enormity of what a single step of faith can do.

> In the movie, Indiana Jones has to pass three supreme tests to reach the Holy Grail and save his father, who is dying.... The third test, the "Path of God," is the most difficult. Indiana comes to the edge of a large chasm—about a hundred feet across and a thousand feet down. On the other side of the chasm is the doorway to the Holy Grail. The instructions read, "Only in the leap from the lion's head will he prove his worth."
>
> Indiana says to himself, "It's impossible. Nobody can jump this." Then he realizes this test requires a leap of faith. His father says, "You must believe, boy. You must believe!" Even though every nerve and fiber of his being screams that he must not do it, Indiana walks to the edge of the cliff, lifts his foot, and then steps out into thin air....
>
> If you've seen the movie, you know what happens next. Indiana does not plummet to his death, but is upheld by an invisible force....

[Indiana] needs only enough faith to take a step. He needs only enough faith to put his life on the line. For the most part, it is a matter of the will. If he is willing to act as if a bridge will be there, the bridge will be there. He will not fall. But he has to take the step first.[12]

The next time fear whispers in your ear, first determine whether it is healthy or unhealthy fear. If it is of the unhealthy variety, don't put up with it. God has given you everything you need to take a stand and take a step.

Whenever we allow
the risen Christ to touch
our areas of profound
disappointment, He
will reappoint us to
something greater.

6

FROM DISAPPOINTMENT TO REAPPOINTMENT

Disappointment occurs when the
actual experience of something falls
far short of what we anticipate.

—PHILIP YANCEY

Sometimes the crystal bowl is not just broken; it is shattered, completely ruined, and beyond repair. Barring a miracle, our frantic efforts to fix it will be a waste of time and energy. Life often leaves us in irreparable situations. When this happens, we experience a wide array of emotions ranging from anger and loss to emptiness and disappointment.

You may have been climbing the company ladder when you suddenly found yourself on the wrong end of corporate downsizing. Perhaps you were an athlete, giving your all, when you blew out a knee, dashing your chances for that athletic scholarship. Or maybe your ex-spouse has moved on with life and is involved in another relationship, but you are still hanging on to hope for reconciliation.

Whatever the reason, you may now find yourself having to deal with disabling disappointment and perhaps even despair and despondence. If so, there is a solution for your situation.

POSITIVE DISAPPOINTMENT

Disappointments are an inevitable part of life. But even our disappointments can produce positive results. God may be using them to reinvent you. Dr. Robert Schuller calls it "absorbing the spills and developing new skills." Sometimes closed doors, failure, and disappointment can become the greatest avenues to blessings. While Dr. Schuller's advice may seem somewhat clichéd, it is exactly the business God is in—the business of turning disappointments into reappointments.[1]

Because of his own failure, Peter was more than a little disappointed. He was devastated, crushed, and humiliated. After faithfully following his Master for more than three years, Peter, in a moment of weakness and cowardice, had denied Him—just as Jesus had predicted—not once, but three times! Peter himself had heard the rooster crow. And once Jesus had been crucified, Peter felt as if his life were over, that there was nothing left to live for. The only solution was to hide out, wallow in his depression, and try to figure out what to do with the mess he'd made of his life.

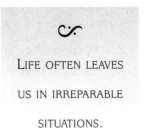

LIFE OFTEN LEAVES US IN IRREPARABLE SITUATIONS.

Then something happened: the resurrection. When Peter came face-to-face with the risen Christ, another miracle happened. Peter the disciple became Peter the apostle. Christ forgave him, healed him, and reappointed him to something greater! Just as He did with Peter, whenever we allow the risen Christ to touch our areas of profound disappointment, He will reappoint us to something greater.

TESSA'S TRIALS

If you were to meet my friend Tessa, you would be drawn to her warm personality, the high degree of intellectual stimulation she offers in conversation, and, especially, her authenticity of spirit. But she has not always been as happy, fulfilled, and successful as she is today. Hers is a story of triumph over disappointment and broken dreams.

When Tessa was thirteen her mother died, leaving a void in her life most children don't have to experience. Fortunately, Tessa had a special aunt who became a pillar in her life. Tessa spent many days and nights visiting her aunt's home. It was a place of love and warmth, filled with delightful aromas forever seeping out from the kitchen and infiltrating the entire house. Tessa's aunt was a stay-at-home mom and a masterful homemaker. Whenever she visited, Tessa would gaze at her aunt from a distance and dream of one day becoming a homemaker just like her, living in a warm and loving home just like hers. As Tessa grew up, that was her vision of how her life would be—of how her life *should* be. She was going to get married, have children, and build a wonderful family home.

EVEN OUR DISAPPOINTMENTS CAN PRODUCE POSITIVE RESULTS.

Tessa did indeed marry her "Prince Charming" and started building her dream home. All went well until her husband became addicted to alcohol and drugs and she found out that he was being unfaithful to her. After Tessa confronted him, he promised to change. Yet the chemical abuse and unfaithfulness continued. Tessa's dreams shattered, and she found herself on her own as a single mom with three children. To make matters worse, she had no career to fall back on because for all her life she had prepared only to be a homemaker. The breakup of her marriage dealt Tessa a crushing blow. She fought frequent bouts of depression and fear and experienced an unhealthy weight loss. Life seemed hopeless. During that time, Tessa wrote a letter to herself that expressed her feelings:

> Tonight, the girls and I decorated the Christmas tree. We spent the evening frolicking around the tree farm in search of that perfect tree with the most fluff. I sampled every one of them and was sure that we had picked the one that smelled the most like Christmas.
>
> Driving home was fun; the girls giggled as we passed cars on the street with our tree sticking two feet out of the trunk of the car. Now, after angel kisses and reprimands for feeding cheddar crackers to Gabby, the dog, they sleep peacefully. I sneaked upstairs to release the tears that I've held back all evening.

This is the second Christmas that the kids and I have spent alone without their daddy. This is the time of year for families, and my heart longs for us to be together. Although that longing is inside of me, I know that my health and my children's future depend upon my being strong. It's a tough fight, but giving in to that longing would just bring more unbearable pain and ultimate destruction. I've learned that doing what's right sometimes means standing alone, and I've found that being alone isn't nearly as painful as being lonely.... Sometimes the anger and hurt overwhelm me.[2]

Because she loved her children and herself, Tessa knew she had to do something. She couldn't continue to live in a pit of despair and poverty. She frantically cried out to God for direction. How would she provide for her children? Where would she find a purpose for her life?

TESSA'S EDUCATION

In the past, Tessa had entertained the idea of teaching school on the elementary level, but she had never had an opportunity to follow her dream. After her divorce, she decided to pursue teaching. The only catch? She would have to attend college. Tessa was in her early thirties with a family to raise. The impossibilities loomed heavily over her. But with humility, great determination, and God's strength, Tessa and her children moved in with her father, and she enrolled in college. "Having a loving and supportive family who helped with the kids and allowed us to stay in their home was a major factor in my recovery process," Tessa told me.

> SOMETIMES CLOSED DOORS, FAILURE, AND DISAPPOINTMENT CAN BECOME THE GREATEST AVENUES TO BLESSINGS.

"Going back to school built up my self-confidence," she continued. "My old dream of being the perfect wife, mother, and homemaker died. It was actually dead long before I was able to let it go. To move forward in a healthy way, I had to develop a new dream."

Tessa knew she had made mistakes, but now she wanted to do more than to avoid the same mistakes. She wanted to thrive. She resolved, "I'm going to find out how to do things right this time." Tessa began a journey to discover a successful and normal life. "If only," she told me, "I could find out what normal was."

Tessa had at that point in her life abandoned the pursuit of a healthy romantic relationship. She had known betrayal, and she never wanted to feel that kind of pain again. She was her own woman now, and with God's help she would find her own way. Tessa's resolve to be a loving mother never changed, but her dream switched from being a perfect homemaker to becoming a successful teacher.

Her grades were high, and she approached her work with diligence and passion. Tessa's confidence soared. "I just knew I was going to be a wonderful teacher. After all, I was attending one of the best elementary education schools in the state, and I had a deep love for children. Who wouldn't want to hire me?"

As Tessa envisioned her future, she pictured a traditional classroom decorated in bright primary colors, with well-mannered children who said, "Good morning, Ms. Tessa!" All of them, smart kids, with caring and involved parents, eager and willing to learn, like little sponges soaking up all the knowledge she would give them.

After graduation, though, Tessa could not find a job. She searched and scoured, but there were no openings. Finally, out of desperation, she interviewed at an inner-city school located in a crime-ridden, drug-infested part of town and was hired to teach the first grade. "It was the only job offered to me, so I had to take it," she told me.

Tessa's Disappointment

When Tessa began teaching, once again her dreams of what life should be shattered. "Most of these kids come to school with no supplies. Their parents are in dire poverty. At first, they didn't want to learn. I had to spend hours teaching them to behave before I could teach them anything else. Many of my students are abused or neglected. Three of my students' parents are in jail. A significant percentage of the kids were crack babies, which causes super-hyperactivity. One of them even brought a gun to school—in the first grade! Another had ringworm patches the size of cup lids all over his body."

> Whenever we allow the risen Christ to touch our areas of profound disappointment, He will reappoint us to something greater.

Each day after work Tessa cried. She bought newspapers and continued diligently to search for a new job. But it was as though a steel door had slammed shut. There were no jobs available. In her desperation Tessa prayed, "God, I can't do this! I went to college for nothing."

Tessa felt like a failure. She had failed first at marriage and now as a teacher. She didn't want to go back into that classroom. "I was driving those around me crazy. Facing each new day became harder and harder, until one day I came to the end of my rope again."

TESSA'S REAPPOINTMENT

That day, after many prayers, a light switched on in Tessa's head. God showed her that she was trying to fit her students into her expectations of what "normal" was supposed to be. With that, Tessa determined not to give up on her job, much less on her students, and to press on. "After a while," she told me, "I began to change. I realized it wasn't the children who needed to change; it was me." She started seeing her students as individuals with individual problems whom God had created and died for. "For some of these kids, I was the only person who offered them any positive emotional support."

Tessa implemented a system in which, at the beginning of each day, each of her students had to greet her by either shaking her hand, slapping her a high five, or giving her a hug. At first, most of the kids were emotionally guarded; too many people in their lives had let them down, and most didn't want anything to do with touching her. Through Tessa's continual praise and the unconditional acceptance she offered, however, they slowly began to open up. Now, almost every one of them gives her not high fives, but hugs. "Some don't want to let me go," Tessa told me. "It may be the only hug they get all day. But they had to learn to trust me."

THERE ARE SOMETIMES SURPRISING RICHES IN THE DETOURS WE ARE FORCED TO TAKE.

Tessa has seen such a change in her students and herself that she now knows that God took her idealistic dream of teaching and turned it into a very realistic calling to reach these children in need. The principal of the school said, "I know God sent Tessa to our school." Tessa responded to the principal's compliment by saying, "Yes, God put me in this school, but it was as much for me as for them." Wow, what a turnaround!

Each of us can apply to our lives the wisdom Tessa gained. Read her words:

> At the end of each day I have peace knowing I'm where God wants me. What

I've learned … is that life is about taking risks. My classroom is not what I envisioned in college and there's always a shortage of funding, but my life is more rewarding than it has ever been. I realized I had to take a leap of faith, which meant trusting people and God again. I know from experience that God can take our broken dreams and unfulfilled expectations and use them if we let Him. Then our lives will be complete.

Most of us desperately want life to fit our ideas of how things should be. We consider a "road closed" sign to be a negative thing. But there are sometimes surprising riches in the detours we are forced to take. Joyce Meyer wrote in her book *Managing Your Emotions*, "[When we are disappointed] we have to make the decision to adapt and adjust, to take a new approach, to just keep going despite our feelings. That's when we must remember that we have the Greater One residing within us, so that no matter what may happen to frustrate us [we can let God turn our disappointment into reappointment]."[3]

I love this concept of letting God reappoint us when life hands us disappointments. My friend Tessa had many disappointments, but in her pain, she let

God reappoint her to a much greater task than she could ever have imagined.

Tessa is thriving on the jagged edges of life. Today she is remarried to a wonderfully supportive and encouraging man. God brought him to her; she wasn't looking. Even in that relationship Tessa has had to learn to let go of her past and trust God again.

The next time you find yourself in a disappointing situation, don't give in to depression and fear. Give in to God and let Him reappoint you.

I would have despaired
unless I had believed that I
would see the goodness of
the LORD in the land of the
living. Wait for the LORD;
be strong and let your heart
take courage; yes, wait for
the LORD.

PSALM 27:13–14 NASB

THE JAGGED EDGE OF WAITING

*Waiting may be the greatest teacher
and trainer in godliness, maturity, and
genuine spirituality most of us
ever encounter.*

—RICHARD HENDRIX

During the course of life we sometimes find ourselves in a situation where we have for so long awaited deliverance that the darkness of despair engulfs us, threatening to crush our hope of ever breaking free. We've wept and cried out to God in frustration, "Lord, I've been waiting on You for so long that I'm exhausted and on the verge of a total breakdown! I can't take it anymore! If You don't come through for me soon, I don't know what I'm going to do. Lord, I must hear from You very soon! Help me, Lord!"

WEIGHTY WAITING

Your issue may be lingering financial pressures. You can't believe you've gotten into this situation. You were sure five years ago that you would havegained your freedom by now. You're a Christian. You love God, but lately the strain has been so great that you've actually entertained thoughts of suicide, thinking that being dead would be a relief. You've prayed, tithed, served God, and can't figure out why He has allowed you to be in this mess. Now, you find yourself drifting into bitterness when you see others prospering. A part of you wants to give up and resign yourself to the idea that things will never change. You believe God when He said in His Word, "Never will I leave you; never will I forsake you" (Heb. 13:5) and "My God will meet all your needs according to his glorious riches in Christ Jesus" (Phil. 4:19). But it certainly *feels* as if God has forgotten you.

It might be that you've been holding on and holding out for that special soul mate—the life partner God has for you. You've been faithful, fighting the temptations that our society constantly throws at you. You've taken a stand, but you've been standing strong so long that your prospects are now as thin as your hairline. You just want a companion, someone to talk to, to share life with, a partner. You feel you'll probably be single your whole life. Bouts of panic and despair have replaced the joyful expectation and faith that once saturated your being.

> ℃
>
> GOD HAS NOT
>
> FORGOTTEN
>
> YOU.

Perhaps you've been the caregiver for a seriously ill or aging loved one. She means the world to you, but caring for her is wearing you down, draining the life from you. You're sleep deprived, fatigued, and emotionally taxed. Weighty decisions are resting squarely on your shoulders. Yet, you can't quit. Someone has to do it. A while back you were sure you couldn't take anymore, that you were going to crack. Now, after the weeks have turned into months and the months into years, you're simply numb, mindlessly going through your daily routine. You are filled with guilt and shame for feeling this way, but you can't help it. You've begun to entertain thoughts of giving up on God.

GOD IS THERE

Whatever the particulars, my friend, be encouraged. You are not alone. Most of us have been in similar situations at one time or another. You are neither unspiritual nor faithless. God has not forgotten you. The psalmist David felt the same way you feel. David learned to handle his fears by applying truth to them. In the pit of his despair he wrote:

> How long, O LORD? Will You forget me
> forever? How long will You hide Your
> face from me? How long shall I take
> counsel in my soul, having sorrow in my
> heart all the day? How long will my
> enemy be exalted over me? ... I am weary
> with my sighing; every night I make my
> bed swim, I dissolve my couch with my
> tears. My eye has wasted away with grief;
> it has become old because of all my
> adversaries.... Why do You stand afar off,
> O LORD? Why do You hide Yourself in
> times of trouble? (Psalm 13:1–2; 6:6–7;
> 10:1 NASB)

Peppered throughout the psalms are candid glimpses of David's humanity that he displayed during his most difficult struggles. I personally relate to David because he had an intense love for God but often felt alienated from Him and ignored by Him. His life was one of breathtaking highs followed by cavernous lows. David knew what it was like to be at the top of his game, but he was also familiar with the hard and unforgiving thud of hitting rock bottom.

God's favor rested powerfully on David when in his youth as a shepherd he killed the lion and the bear that had attacked his sheep. Then, to the surprise of David's brothers, the prophet Samuel anointed him as the future king of Israel. God's anointing on his life soon began to manifest itself when David played the harp for King Saul. His music brought Saul great emotional relief and moved other listeners to worship. Then, against enormous odds, he killed the great Philistine warrior Goliath and overnight became a national hero. Instead of reveling in arrogance, though, he gave the credit to God and humbly submitted himself to King Saul as his loyal servant. David would see his anointing bring forth great results as God honored his faith. He became Saul's armor bearer, a captain in the army, and a musician in the royal court. David was

> DAVID KNEW WHAT IT WAS LIKE TO BE AT THE TOP OF HIS GAME, BUT HE WAS ALSO FAMILIAR WITH THE HARD AND UNFORGIVING THUD OF HITTING ROCK BOTTOM.

a rising star in the kingdom of Saul. He followed
God's will and was doing all the right things for the
right reasons.

WAITING ON THE RUN

We'd expect God would continue to pour out His
blessings on David until the appointed time to usher
him into his role of king. That's what we'd expect
for a righteous servant whom God had dubbed a
man after His own heart, wouldn't we? But David
experienced the exact opposite. Just as quickly as
he'd become a hero, David found himself ruthlessly
cast out of the very kingdom he was destined to
lead. First Samuel 18:6–9 tells the story:

> When the men were returning home after
> David had killed the Philistine, the
> women came out from all the towns of
> Israel to meet King Saul with singing and
> dancing, with joyful songs and with tam-
> bourines and lutes. As they danced, they
> sang: "Saul has slain his thousands, and
> David his tens of thousands." Saul was
> very angry; this refrain galled him. "They
> have credited David with tens of thou-
> sands," he thought, "but me with only
> thousands. What more can he get but the

kingdom?" And from that time on Saul kept a jealous eye on David.

The Bible goes on to say that an evil spirit entered Saul, and he eventually

sent men to David's house to watch it and to kill him in the morning. But Michal, David's wife, warned him, "If you don't run for your life tonight, tomorrow you'll be killed." So Michal let David down through a window, and he fled and escaped.... Then David fled ... and went to Jonathan [David's best friend and Saul's son] and asked, "What have I done? What is my crime? How have I wronged your father, that he is trying to take my life?" (1 Samuel 19:11–12; 20:1)

ↄ

DAVID KNEW IT WAS WORTH-WHILE TO WAIT ON GOD, EVEN WHEN HE DIDN'T UNDER-STAND THE DELAYS.

Saul's armed forces hunted David for years, as if he were an escaped convict. The future king was a fugitive on the run, hiding in caves, forests, and mountains—any place he could find to stay alive. Biblical commentator F. B. Meyer wrote, "Saul's persecutions lasted for eight to nine years; and no hope of termination appeared. David was a man who spends five hundred days passing through a forest. The tangled over-growth hides the sun; and he begins to despair of ever emerging."[1]

WHEN WE HAVE BEEN WAITING ON GOD FOR DELIVERANCE, A PROLONGED DELAY BECOMES A SHARP AND JAGGED EDGE IN OUR LIVES.

David was on the run in the wilderness, not for several days or weeks, but for eight to nine years! David at one point took up residence in the cave of Adullam. The thought of David living in that cave reminds me of the news reports of the terrorist Osama Bin Laden hiding out in the mountains and caves of Afghanistan. I imagine the territory where David hid was of similar topography—rough, jagged, and unpleasant.

When news got out about David being on the run from Saul, about four hundred men joined him at the cave. That number eventually grew to six hundred, still a relatively small number compared to Saul's army of thousands. In addition to their small number, the Bible describes the men who joined

THE JAGGED EDGE OF WAITING   119

David as "everyone who was discontented" (1 Sam. 22:2 NKJV). The Hebrew word translated *discontented* is a combination of the words *marah* and *nephesh*, meaning literally "bitter in spirit."[2] David's followers were bitter people—not exactly the pick of the litter! They would repeatedly offer him worldly counsel, advising him at every opportunity to kill Saul! David refused to take their advice, which caused his men to misunderstand and question him. His actions often upset and infuriated them. The men grew impatient and couldn't understand why David wouldn't take control and decisively bring an end to Saul's harassment. But David was waiting for God to deliver him, even though he could have, in his own power, ended his problems with Saul. David knew it was worthwhile to wait on God, even when he didn't understand the delays.

The same holds true for us. Our human nature urges us, saying, "Don't just *stand* there, *do* something!" As Henry Blackaby noted, however, God often says to us, "Don't just do something, but stand there!"[3] That is precisely what David was doing while he was waiting and running.

During those years of flight from Saul, David composed some of his most heartfelt psalms. Many of them are simply desperate pleas to God for help. When I examine David's prayers, I find solace—even if I don't find answers—because I realize I am not alone.

God had promised David that he would be king of Israel, but instead of seeing fulfillment, he was seeing the exact opposite, with not even a hint of change on the horizon. David frequently cried out to God, "How long?" He had been waiting on God for so long that his eyes were starting to fail. This means that David was rapidly losing strength from the waiting associated with his continual grief, unfulfilled longings, and delayed hope. David would agree that, when we have been waiting on God for deliverance, a prolonged delay becomes a sharp and jagged edge in our lives. Our strength begins to fade, and we become weak in body and spirit. We feel forgotten, frustrated, discouraged, isolated, and even forsaken. It must have seemed to David that his life and ministry were going to waste, that he was squandering his best years, and that despite his prayers, nothing was happening.

WE MAY NOT SEE IT, BUT, AS WE WAIT ON GOD, A GREAT DEAL IS HAPPENING.

The sense that nothing is happening is one of the main reasons waiting on God is so difficult. Regardless of our pleas and cries to Him, it appears that God is not listening or even hearing. As time passes, doubt slowly but steadily chips away at our faith, eroding it like the wind and rain erode a canyon.

We may not see it, but, as we wait on God, a great deal is happening. We fail to notice what He's doing because our spiritual sight is blurred by our pain. Isaiah 64:4 (NLT) makes no bones about it. God is at work for us even as we wait on Him: "For since the world began, no ear has heard, and no eye has seen a God like you, who works for those who wait for him!" God is in fact working during the long, confusing delays in our lives. And as we previously pointed out, He knows the individual hairs on our heads, even while we are waiting.

Consider for a moment another Old Testament figure with whom many of us are familiar.

WAITING IN PRISON

Joseph, the son of Jacob, is an example of one who experienced delays in the fulfillment of God's promises to him. Joseph, like David, was strong, capable, and sharp. He, too, had a heart for God and walked in obedience and faith. From Joseph's youth, God manifested Himself to him by revealing his destiny. He would one day become a great ruler whom God would use in a mighty way. Before he ever received the divine scepter, however, Joseph's own brothers betrayed him and sold him into slavery. Nevertheless, Joseph didn't lose faith, but continued to trust God. As a result, he was promoted to become his master's number one slave in charge of his whole house.

Everything was going great for Joseph until one day when he came face-to-face with the opportunity to sleep with his master Potiphar's wife when she tried to seduce him. Being the full-blooded male that he undoubtedly was, the magnetism was strong. Joseph, however, resisted temptation, called out to God, and fled the scene. He chose to do the right thing.

And the reward for his honorable, godly response? There was no parade or even recognition for Joseph. Instead Potiphar's wife framed him, and Joseph soon found himself with yet another address, this one on Penitentiary Lane. There sat Joseph, at the zenith of what should have been his most productive period, holding on to the promise of God, but wasting away in prison—for possibly up to ten years!

None of this makes sense to the natural mind. It's like a professional coach who benches his best player during the prime of his career! But God operates from a different perspective and on a separate timetable from ours. There was a divine purpose behind Joseph's imprisonment, though. I'm sure there were times when in that cold, dirty, and dark prison cell when Joseph felt confused, useless, and depressed—especially as the months dragged into years.

Here's another truth to chew on. It wasn't Satan who put Joseph in that prison. It was *God*. He allowed Joseph's brothers to mistreat him. God, in order to bring about His higher purpose, permitted others to wrongfully accuse him. Joseph told his brothers after saving them and revealing his identity to them, "Do not be distressed and do not be angry with yourselves for selling me here, because it was to save lives that God sent me ahead of you.... God sent me ahead of you to preserve for you a remnant on earth and to save your lives by a great deliverance. So then, it was not you who sent me here, but God" (Gen. 45:5, 7–8). On another occasion Joseph told his brothers, "You intended to harm me, but God intended it for good to accomplish what is now being done, the saving of many lives" (50:20).

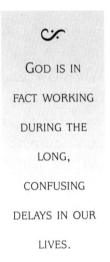

GOD IS IN FACT WORKING DURING THE LONG, CONFUSING DELAYS IN OUR LIVES.

There are many other prominent biblical figures who had to wait long periods of time for God to act on their behalf. For example, although God promised Abraham that he would have a son, Abraham's wife, Sarah, was barren so they had to depend totally on God to fulfill what He had promised. Abraham and Sarah waited decades for the birth of Isaac, the child of promise. Then there was Job. God allowed him to be afflicted by Satan. Satan was the afflicter, but God allowed it. Next consider Moses. God sent him into the desert for forty years in order to let Moses die to himself so God could eventually use him in a greater capacity. And it was God who arranged David's decade of cave dwelling.

WAITING TO PREPARE

When God allows us to go through prolonged periods of waiting and delay, sometimes all we can do is seek God's face, surrender to Him, and wait for His good purpose to unfold: "I would have despaired unless I had believed that I would see the goodness of the LORD in the land of the living. Wait for the LORD; be strong and let your heart take courage; yes, wait for the LORD" (Ps. 27:13–14 NASB).

But when we are living in prison, a cave, or a desert, it's often hard to see this. Especially when we don't understand God's plans. In Joseph's and David's cases, their hearts required preparation for the greater purpose God had envisioned. God has a purpose for you, too. He's not just preparing you to be "successful." He has something for you to do for Him here on earth as well as someday in heaven. He may see a person here on earth that only *you* will be able to reach. God may be using your circumstances to put you in a position to reach that one person.

Then there's what He'll have you do in heaven. Despite all the Hollywood stereotypes, heaven is not a place where people sit around on clouds, strumming harps. We will be serving and working in God's kingdom for all eternity. It's a big universe, and God is a creative God, so there's no telling what He'll have us doing. Everything we're going through now is preparation for that work. The truth is, God has you where you are because He loves you and is refining you. God's purpose is to bring forth from your hardship a profound blessing. Remember, Romans 8:28 plainly declares that "in *all* things God works for the good of those who love him, who have been called according to his purpose."

But we sometimes bring trouble on ourselves. While attending seminary, I worked part-time for a

WHEN GOD ALLOWS US TO GO THROUGH PROLONGED PERIODS OF WAITING AND DELAY, SOMETIMES ALL WE CAN DO IS SEEK GOD'S FACE, SURRENDER TO HIM, AND WAIT FOR HIS GOOD PURPOSE TO UNFOLD.

large package-delivery company, and my job was to load the trucks before the drivers came in. The job paid well and was coveted by many students. One guy, zealous for the Lord, was always witnessing on the job. Now, I'm certainly in favor of presenting an appropriate witness at work, but we must always take care that it doesn't interfere with our tasks. The fellow I'm talking about constantly fell behind on his job because he wouldn't stop talking about the Lord. As you can guess, they eventually fired him.

Afterward, he had financial difficulty and complained to everyone at school that he had been persecuted because of his faith. No, he was fired because he wasn't a good worker and was in the prison of financial difficulty because of his own folly.

On the other hand, it's possible to find ourselves in a painful situation when we've done nothing wrong or foolish but are simply obeying God. God sometimes allows His children to live in difficult circumstances so we can have a platform from which to speak into the lives of other hurting people. Psalm 84:5–6 declares, "Blessed are those whose strength is in you, who have set their hearts

GOD'S PURPOSE IS TO BRING FORTH FROM YOUR HARDSHIP A PROFOUND BLESSING.

on pilgrimage. As they [God's people] pass through the Valley of Baca [weeping], they make it a place of springs." What does a spring do? It refreshes people. God may be allowing you to go through your hardship so you can bring refreshment to other people.

I can almost hear someone saying, "But I didn't do anything wrong to warrant the situation I'm in." You must understand, you may be in your current circumstance because of what you've done *right!* You desire to know God on a deeper level. You've prayed for Him to increase your effectiveness. Maybe He's answering your request. Read what Psalm 105 says about Joseph's life: "He [God] called down famine on the land and destroyed all their supplies of food; and he sent a man before them—Joseph, sold as a slave. They bruised his feet with shackles, his neck was put in irons, till what he foretold came to pass, till the word of the LORD proved him true" (vv. 16–19).

God is the same in the twenty-first century as He was in Joseph's day. There are seasons in our lives when God allows famine to touch us. It could be physical or spiritual—a season when we seem to be starving for more of God. God used the famine in Egypt to further His purposes. He stirs up our hunger to know Him more by allowing us to experience spiritual famines for a season.

God had given Joseph a dream: "Joseph had a dream, and when he told it to his brothers, they hated him all the more. He said to them, 'Listen to this dream I had: We were binding sheaves of grain out in the field when suddenly my sheaf rose and stood upright, while your sheaves gathered around mine and bowed down to it'" (Gen. 37:5–7). Joseph was destined for a greatness that would serve God's purposes.

> GOD MAY BE ALLOWING YOU TO GO THROUGH YOUR HARDSHIP SO YOU CAN BRING REFRESHMENT TO OTHER PEOPLE.

In his heart, Joseph held on to the dream God gave him, and his faith was tried "till what he foretold came to pass, till the word of the LORD proved him true" (Ps. 105:19). Joseph's faith was tried with ten to fifteen years of waiting and delays, of mistreatment and imprisonment. Some have taught that when Joseph was young, he mouthed off to his brothers about his dreams when he should have just kept his mouth shut. There may be some truth in that statement, but he was also declaring what he believed God would do. But then the great delay came and after a few years in prison, I suspect Joseph entertained thoughts like, *I wonder if I missed God. Maybe those dreams were just my own imagination. I must have been delusional to think that God was really speaking to me.*

Waiting to Train

When I was a senior in high school, I felt strongly that God had spoken to my heart that I was going to be an author. In my innermost being, I believed it was God and proceeded to alter my path in order to walk in obedience. After holding that word in my heart for more than twenty years with no sign of its fulfillment, I began to wonder if I had really heard God. Friends would ask, "When are you going to get a *real* job?" Some people subtly communicated a "what gives you the authority to write books?" attitude.

I eventually saw that God was using the years and bruising circumstances to make me a better writer. The more life experiences I worked through, the more credibility my writing had. Even devastating hardships like dealing with James' deafness, going through a painful divorce while pastoring a church twelve years ago, and hitting financial rock bottom, were all tools God used to give me a platform to speak into people's lives. He allowed me to go through difficult times of waiting to promote His purpose in me.

By the time of Joseph's release from prison, he was a completely different man. No longer was he the impulsive guy who needed to divulge all he was envisioning and perceiving. God had used this time of waiting to cultivate in Joseph a quiet confidence that prepared him to rule over Egypt and his brothers with humility and grace. This is what God desires to cultivate in us also: "The effect of righteousness will be quietness and confidence forever" (Isa. 32:17).

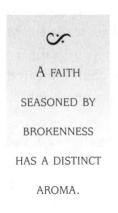

A FAITH SEASONED BY BROKENNESS HAS A DISTINCT AROMA.

The fulfillment of Joseph's dream began to fall into place when Pharaoh had a prophetic dream that none of his oracles could interpret. At about the same time, Pharaoh's chief butler recalled that, when he was in prison, Joseph had accurately interpreted one of his dreams. Pharaoh dispatched guards to bring Joseph to him. After spending more than a decade in prison, Joseph found himself standing before Pharaoh.

When Pharaoh described his dream, Joseph immediately interpreted it. Through his godly wisdom, Joseph was also able to offer Pharaoh a specific plan for responding to the emergency the dream foretold. Joseph told Pharaoh:

"And now let Pharaoh look for a discerning
and wise man and put him in charge of the
land of Egypt. Let Pharaoh appoint com-
missioners over the land to take a fifth of
the harvest of Egypt during the seven years
of abundance. They should collect all the
food of these good years that are coming
and store up the grain under the authority
of Pharaoh, to be kept in the cities for
food. This food should be held in reserve
for the country, to be used during the
seven years of famine that will come upon
Egypt, so that the country may not be
ruined by the famine." The plan seemed
good to Pharaoh and to all his officials. So
Pharaoh asked them, "Can we find anyone
like this man, one in whom is the spirit of
God?" Then Pharaoh said to Joseph,
"Since God has made all this known to
you, there is no one so discerning and wise
as you. You shall be in charge of my palace,
and all my people are to submit to your
orders. Only with respect to the throne will
I be greater than you." (Genesis 41:33–40)

God established Joseph in Egypt and blessed him
with a wife named Asenath and two sons. The names
Joseph chose for his sons were a tribute to God's

activity in his life: "Joseph named his firstborn Manasseh and said, 'It is because God has made me forget all my trouble and all my father's household.' The second son he named Ephraim and said, 'It is because God has made me fruitful in the land of my suffering'" (Gen. 41:51–52).

As with Joseph, God sent David into the wasteland for ten years in order to train him. David already had great faith. He was the only man in the whole of Israel with the courage to go head-to-head with the great Philistine warrior Goliath. "David said to the Philistine, 'You come against me with sword and spear and javelin, but I come against you in the name of the LORD Almighty, the God of the armies of Israel, whom you have defied. This day the LORD will hand you over to me'" (1 Sam. 17:45–46).

David already possessed a giant-slaying faith, but it was the faith of a courageous but *untrained* recruit. God would use the wilderness as a tool to train and season David's faith. Just as a trainer breaks a fine stallion and harnesses him for maximum usefulness, God would also "break" David. A fine stallion may look majestic as it runs wild on the open range, but until it has been broken it is virtually useless. Until we are broken, we cannot realize our full potential. Once a stallion is broken, it requires regular training. You and I may require repeated "breakings." And with each experience of brokenness, God continues to train us and to move us to a higher level of usefulness. Just as God used the waiting and delays to break and train David and Joseph, He uses similar circumstances to break and train us.

FRAGRANT FAITH

A faith seasoned by brokenness has a distinct aroma. It's the fragrance of quiet confidence, grace, and mercy. Broken people don't need to manipulate circumstances or other people, because their assurance rests in God's sovereignty alone. Faith seasoned by brokenness has been forged in the kiln of adversity and has the grit to hold strong under pressure.

After many more trials and battles, God, at His appointed time, delivered Israel to David, who throughout the years of delay never let go of his trust in God. On two separate occasions David spared Saul's life. He could easily have killed the king, but he refused to take matters into his own hands. David chose instead to trust God for his deliverance. David knew what it meant to trust God on the jagged edge!

Jim Cymbala explained it well in his book *Fresh Faith:*

The hardest part of faith is often simply to
wait. And the trouble is, if we don't, then
we start to fix the problem ourselves—and
that makes it worse.

We complicate the situation to the
point where it takes God much longer to
fix it than if we had quietly waited for his
working in the first place.

The timing of God is often a mystery
to us, and even sometimes a frustration.
But we must not give up. We must not
try to arrange our own solutions.
Instead, we must keep on believing and
waiting for God. We will not be alone as
we patiently wait for His answer in His
time. We will be joining the great hosts
of saints down through the ages whose
faith was tested and purified by waiting
for God.[4]

WHEN EVIL
APPEARS TO
TRIUMPH

*Outside of the resurrection of Jesus, I do
not know of any other hope for the world.*

—KONRAD ADENAUER,
FORMER CHANCELLOR OF WEST GERMANY,
IMPRISONED BY ADOLF HITLER FOR
OPPOSING THE NAZI REGIME

I recently watched a television interview with one
of the world's leading scientists. The scientist
seemed well mannered and pleasant, not vindictive
at all toward people of faith. She had come to the
conclusion that science was not a hindrance to faith
in God and that it often supports such faith. As she

was making her point, however, she nonchalantly
mentioned that she was an atheist. The interviewer,
somewhat surprised, said, "Hold on a second. Let's
go back to what I thought you just said. Did you say
you were an atheist?"

"Yes, I did," she responded politely.

"You're telling us that science lends support to
God, and yet you are an atheist. That doesn't make
sense."

The scientist's next response was honest and
revealing. "Oh, I'm not an atheist because of science," she said. "I'm an atheist because of all the evil
and suffering in the world. I can't imagine a God
that would allow the Holocaust, war, and the torture
and starvation of millions of innocent people. If God
is a God of love," she continued, "He would not
allow that. He would step in and put a stop to it."

A sad expression then fell across her face, as if she
had some deep unfulfilled longing in her heart for
something more. "If anything," she said, "science
gives me some hope that there may be a God. I
would like to believe, but I just can't. Faith is a gift
I would love to have."

This woman was simply being honest. My heart
went out to her.

The Greek philosopher Epicurus (341–270 BC)
once asked, "Is [God] willing to prevent evil, but
unable to do so? Then he is impotent. Is he able but

unwilling? Then [God] is malevolent. Is he both willing and able? Whence, then is evil?"[1]

On the surface, Epicurus's questions may seem unanswerable. Why does God allow evil to persist and, so often, to triumph?

I recall hearing of a beautiful, bright-eyed, nine-year-old girl, full of life and love, who was abducted from her home, sexually molested, and then brutally murdered. The man charged with the crime confessed to it and led police to her body. He was a registered sex offender with a record of twenty-four prior arrests!

Try to imagine you have the unthinkable task of explaining to the young girl's parents why God allowed this horrible tragedy. There are two approaches you might take. On the one hand, you could callously tell the parents that this tragedy has happened because of some sin in their lives. I can almost hear your reaction: "Get real; nobody would actually tell someone that." Don't bet on it. We Christians can say some pretty stupid things.

WE HAVE A GREAT GOD WHO DOESN'T CAUSE TRAGEDIES, BUT WHO IS ABLE TO USE THEM FOR OUR GOOD.

A precious Christian couple started attending my church. When they came to us, they were devastated by the recent loss of their infant son to Sudden Infant Death Syndrome (SIDS). They were equally devastated by the counsel they had received at their previous church. Their pastor told them, "You obviously did not pray a hedge completely around your family and allowed Satan to come in and steal your child." Then he quoted John 10:10 (KJV): "The thief cometh not, but for to steal, and to kill, and to destroy: I am come that they might have life, and that they might have it more abundantly." The thief Satan is undoubtedly a real and present adversary. But it is possible to do all the right things—to pray, to "bind" the Enemy, to put on God's armor, and to "cover" our families—and still hear evil knocking at our front door. Is it because God has dropped the ball? To some it may appear so.

> JESUS WAS MORE EAGER TO CHANGE AND REDEEM LIVES THAN HE WAS TO EXPLAIN WHY EVIL THINGS HAPPENED IN THOSE LIVES.

Another way to approach the parents of the murdered girl would be to smile brightly and tell the parents that the pointless tragedy is something for which they should be grateful because it's a divine occasion for them to learn and build their character.

A "mature" Christian once told me that God had sent me a deaf son to keep me humble in my ministry. As if God looked down on my situation and said to Himself, "I need to keep Max humble. So despite all the suffering his son will have to endure, I will allow James to be deaf."

God doesn't work that way. It is true that God will take anything, even senseless tragedies, and use them for our good. Am I more humble because of James' deafness? Absolutely. But that humility is a result of God's desire to *use* trials in our lives, not to *abuse* us with trials! He uses everything for His purposes. I don't believe, however, that God actually causes these things. God does not cause kids to be abducted and murdered just so He can teach us something. The better perspective is that we have a great God who doesn't cause tragedies, but who is able to use them for our good.

How, then, do we answer the question of evil in the world? More important, how do we respond to it? In answering these two questions, we need to start with the second question first. How do we respond to evil when it appears to triumph?

DEALING WITH EVIL

The proper response to evil is to examine how Christ Himself responded to it. Whenever Christ,

who was God incarnate, came face-to-face with pain
or evil, He never felt the need to explain it or apologize for it. He simply dealt with it. When Jesus
encountered people possessed by demons, He
didn't debate the demons. He just cast them out.
When Jesus met a man born blind and His disciples
asked Him whose sin had caused the blindness, He
said that nobody had sinned, that God had allowed
the man to be born blind in order to display the
power of God in his life (see John 9:1–3 NASB).
Jesus never debated about the unfairness that
existed between the classes of society. He simply
said, "The poor you will always have with you"
(Mark 14:7), then He ministered to them. To those
unfortunate few in society who had contracted the
dreaded disease of leprosy, He never explained why
they were ill. He just loved them, brought life to
them, and healed them. Those who were oppressed
and in bondage, He set free.

Jesus lived with the knowledge that evil does in
fact exist and that Satan is real. He never questioned
it. Christ simply did what His Father sent Him here
to do—to deal with it. He said, "The Spirit of the
Lord is on me, because he has anointed me to preach
good news to the poor. He has sent me to proclaim
freedom for the prisoners and recovery of sight for
the blind, to release the oppressed, to proclaim the
year of the Lord's favor" (Luke 4:18–19).

On one occasion a number of Galileans had been cruelly murdered by Pilate even as they were in the act of making their sacrifices to God. This was a particularly monstrous act of evil committed by a monster of a man. Matthew Henry's commentary indicates that these Galileans, when they offered their animal sacrifices, had unwittingly broken some Roman regulation. As a result, Pilate had them slaughtered.

A group of Pharisees, questioning why God had allowed this to happen, felt sure it was due to some sin the Galileans had committed. They also saw it as an opportunity to trap Jesus with a trick question. But Jesus answered, "Do you think that these Galileans were worse sinners than all the other Galileans because they suffered this way? I tell you, no!" (Luke 13:2–3). Jesus was saying, "Everyone is sinful and in need of God. Everyone misses the mark of perfection, and these Galileans didn't do anything especially wrong to cause this terrible suffering to

GOD'S STRATEGY FOR DEALING WITH EVIL WAS TO SEND HIS SON INTO THE MIDDLE OF IT AND TO DEFEAT IT, TO BREAK THE POWER OF SIN IN THE WORLD, AND TO RECONCILE PEOPLE TO HIMSELF THROUGH JESUS.

befall them." It was a result of living in a fallen, sin-inundated world where evil flourishes.

In order to illustrate His point further, Jesus brought up another tragic event: "Or those eighteen who died when the tower in Siloam fell on them—do you think they were more guilty than all the others living in Jerusalem? I tell you, no!" (Luke 13:4–5). Jesus didn't apologize for the existence of evil or for the bad things that happen. Those things were not His focus. His attention was always on His purpose, which was to breathe new life into dead situations and to bring life to people who were spiritually dead.

> GOD IS ABLE TO WORK GOOD IN "ALL" SITUATIONS, EVEN IN THOSE EXCEEDINGLY PAINFUL CIRCUMSTANCES IN WHICH THE GOOD IS ABSENT AND EVIL SEEMS TO TRIUMPH.

After Jesus addressed the Siloam accident, He told the Pharisees, "But unless you repent, you too will all perish" (v. 5). Jesus was being strong here because He knew the hardness of the Pharisees' hearts. But He was also extending an invitation to spiritual rebirth. Jesus was asserting to them that, yes, bad things happen, and we are all under the curse of sin. He was also imploring them to recognize that unless each of us repents and receives new life, we will remain under sin's curse. Jesus was more eager to change and redeem lives than He was to explain why evil things happened in those lives.

God's strategy for dealing with evil was to send His Son into the middle of it and to defeat it, to break the power of sin in the world, and to reconcile people to Himself through Jesus. When Jesus hung on that cross and died, it appeared that evil had triumphed and Satan had won. But then, out of the ashes of defeat, God manifested His power, and Christ rose from the grave, conquering the power of evil and death once and for all.

After Jesus' resurrection, God would send the Holy Spirit to infuse the lives of believers with power. Shortly before His death, Jesus told His disciples, "I tell you the truth: It is for your good that I am going away. Unless I go away, the Counselor [Holy Spirit] will not come to you; but if I go, I will send him to you" (John 16:7).

The purpose of the Holy Spirit's coming and abiding in us is to make it possible for us to live in communion with God: "We have not received the spirit of the world but the Spirit who is from God, that we may understand what God has freely given us. This is what we speak, not in words taught us by human wisdom but in words taught by the Spirit, expressing spiritual truths in spiritual words" (1 Cor. 2:12–13).

Another purpose of the Holy Spirit in our lives is to empower us to become partners with God in redeeming this world. Jesus said, "You will receive power when the Holy Spirit comes on you" (Acts 1:8). One aspect of our partnership with God in redeeming the world is the role He assigns to us in fulfilling the Great Commission—to be witnesses for Christ wherever God has placed us (see Matt. 28:16–20). The other aspect of our partnership in redeeming the world is to face and deal with evil in the same manner Jesus did.

> ∾
>
> GOD ALLOWS EVIL TO EXIST BECAUSE GOD'S WORK IS NOT YET FINISHED, AND HE CALLS US TO SHARE IN HIS REDEMPTIVE WORK.

Consider this: God's work as the Maker and Designer of the universe involved the creation of something out of nothing. Scientists to this day, even with all the available technology, are unable to create one single molecule of matter. We can do wonders with the matter that already exists. We can reshape it, break it down, and change its form. But we are unable either to create it or destroy it. Scientists have yet to figure out exactly how matter came into existence. Just as God formed matter out of nothing in His creation of the universe, His role as Redeemer in our lives involves the creation of something good where formerly there was nothing good. This is why the Christ follower can stand with confidence on Romans 8:28: "And we know that in all things God works for the good of those who love him." Notice the little word *all*. God is able to work good in "all" situations, even in those exceedingly painful circumstances in which the good is absent and evil seems to triumph. God can create something good where good doesn't exist.

God allows evil to exist because God's work is not yet finished, and He calls us to share in His redemptive work. Romans 12:21 exhorts us, "Do not be overcome by evil, but overcome evil with good." God has commissioned us to carry out His work. Part of our mission is, through the Holy Spirit's power, to overcome evil with good—to partner with God in the creation of something good where evil now resides. Notice that I'm not saying there's a little bit of good in everything—even in evil—for which we should look. No. I'm talking about how God takes evil and by His power *transforms* it into something good. There's a big difference.

THE PRESENCE OF EVIL

Then there is the question, "Why does God even allow evil to exist?" The answer relates at least in part to our partnership with God in redeeming this evil world. When God created the universe out of nothing, the apex of this creation was man. Unlike the rest of nature, God created man in His own image. To bear God's image refers in part to the ability to reason, to create, to be self-aware, to have regard for others, and the ability to give and receive love. It also speaks of free will.

LOVE IS MESSY.

God wanted beings who would willingly join Him in a loving relationship and who would work with Him in partnership. He wanted them to enjoy free will. To force love or a change of heart would pervert those beings into mere machines. For love to be possible there must be freedom of choice. In order to choose to love, we must likewise be able to choose *not* to love and to follow evil. There cannot be a positive without a negative. It is impossible. God knew that in order to endow human beings with free will, capable of reciprocal love, evil would also have to exist; therefore, suffering and injustice would exist as evil's natural by-products.

God could have stepped in, exercised His authority, and put a stop to evil and suffering. But at what cost? It would have cost us our free will and the ability to love freely. The truth is, love is messy.

When we get close to a person, we see both their good points and their bad points. Wherever there is true love there is always risk and the possibility of getting hurt. The same holds true with love on a much grander scale. God loved us so much that He gave us free will to choose whether we would love Him in return. If He took away evil and suffering, He would have to take away from us that choice. God evidently thought creating beings capable of love and free will was worth the risk and the price. I like the way John Eldredge described it in his book *Epic:*

> God gives us the freedom to reject him. He gives to each of us a will of our own. Good grief, why? ... He knows how we will use our freedom, what misery and suffering, what hell will be unleashed on earth because of our choices. Why? Is he out of his mind?
>
> The answer is as simple and staggering as this: if you want a world where love is real, you must allow each person the freedom to choose.... Any parent or lover knows this: love is chosen. You cannot, in the end, force anyone to love you.
>
> So if you are writing a story where love is the meaning, where love is the

highest and best of all, where love is the
point, then you have to allow each person
a choice. You have to allow freedom. You
cannot force love. God gives us the dig-
nity of freedom, to choose for or against
him.[2]

Philip Yancey put it this way in his book
Disappointment with God:

Power can do everything but the most
important thing: it cannot
control love.... In a concentration camp, the guards
possess almost unlimited
power. By applying force,
they can make you renounce
your God, curse your family,
work without pay, eat
human excrement, kill and
then bury your closest
friend or even your own
mother. All this is within
their power. Only one thing
is not: they cannot force
you to love them. This fact may help
explain why God sometimes seems shy to

> GOD WILL, IN FACT, STEP IN AND PUT A COMPLETE AND FINAL STOP TO ALL EVIL AND SUFFERING.

use his power. He created us to love
him, but his most impressive displays of
miracles—the kind we may secretly long
for—do nothing to foster that love. As
Douglas John Hall has put it, "God's
problem is not that God is not able to
do certain things. God's problem is that
God loves. Love complicates the life of
God as it complicates every life."[3]

To answer the scientist at the beginning of this
chapter: God allows evil to exist in the world now
because of His love for us and because His work is
not yet finished. One day, however, it will be finished, and God will, in fact, step in and put a
complete and final stop to all evil and suffering.
"God will wipe away every tear from their eyes;
there shall be no more death, nor sorrow, nor crying. There shall be no more pain" (Rev. 21:4 NKJV).
But we are at present called to be in relationship
with God as His children and to partner with Him
in His redemptive work. This means living in a
world that is incomplete and imperfect. It means
allowing God to create good in situations where
nothing good is present and evil abounds.

Heather Gemmen's story is an example of how
God creates good where only evil existed. A stranger

broke into her home, brutally raped her, and as a result, she became pregnant. She experienced all the emotional grief and devastation that anyone in that situation would. She, too, cried out to God in anguish. Yet, though she was a victim, Heather chose to throw away the victim mentality, to embrace the struggle, and to turn her pain over to God, releasing His power to create something good where there was only evil. Heather and her husband later made another series of difficult choices: to carry the baby to term and embrace the child as their own. Read her understanding of God's work in her life from her book *Startling Beauty:*

> Rape is ugliness at its basest form. Rape destroys innocence and cultivates bitterness. It steals security and extends fear. It kills hope and fosters shame. Rape leaves no room for beauty.... Rape takes too much. But I, for one, have gained more than I have lost. I have been startled by beauty in places it doesn't belong. I see it on a bloodied cross, and bitterness loses its power. I see it on the faces of those who keep their promises to me, and fear releases its grip. I see it in the graceful dance of a child who was so unwanted, and hope revives its song.[4]

Heather has known how evil sometimes seems to triumph. Yet, she also knows that God has not abandoned her, that He hurts with her, and that He can take the most horrifying evil and create something good. You may have suffered unjustly in some way. Or maybe your children have. Jesus came to bring healing and peace to an evil world. In that place where evil overwhelms, He can create hope and beauty.

If only for this life we
have hope in Christ,
we are to be pitied
more than all men.

1 CORINTHIANS 15:19

The Battle for Our Minds

*It is the Lord's purpose for our life that we
be free from every yoke but one—His
yoke.... The ultimate freedom comes from
knowing the truth—the truth of who He is
and where He sits above all rule and
authority and dominion. To know the truth
is to live by it, and to live by it is to demonstrate it. If we say we believe the truth but
do not live by it, we only deceive ourselves.*

—Rick Joyner

Wherever I speak—regardless of the size of the
group, its location, or the economic status of those in

attendance—there are always several people who, in need of ministry and counsel, pour out their heartrending stories to me. I've become acutely aware that a considerable percentage of those in my audience are undergoing some type of distressing trial.

Somewhere near the end of my presentation, I'll take a deep breath and say something like, "Folks, let's get real here. Either God is real, Jesus was in fact raised from the dead, and heaven is our eternal home or we're all just a bunch of fools chasing some fantasy to soothe our consciences. If that's the case, then we should all just go home and eat, drink, and be merry, because we're wasting our time." Then I read 1 Corinthians 15:19: "If only for this life we have hope in Christ, we are to be pitied more than all men." In other words, Paul was saying, "Hey, guys, if we came to Christ to have a grand ol' time in this life, then we are all a bunch of idiots, because the moment we became Christ followers, our lives really started to get messy." Why, Paul and every one of the other apostles, except John who was exiled, were eventually martyred! As a result of Paul's newfound faith, he spent half his life in and out of prison, and ended up being beheaded.

STRUCK DOWN, BUT NOT DESTROYED

During the rule of Emperor Nero in the first century, thousands upon thousands of Christians were tortured to death. The Roman historian Tacitus wrote that Christians "died in torments, and their torments were embittered by insult and derision. Some were nailed on crosses; others sewn up in the skins of wild beasts and exposed to the fury of dogs; others, again, smeared over with combustible materials, were used as torches to illuminate the darkness of the night."[1]

Today Christians all over the globe are living in persecution or poverty, and many are dying for their faith. Several years ago when I was a pastor, my wife and I hosted an African pastor and his family in our home. Their country had once been free, and his church had flourished. Then, overnight, a communist regime took over. One of the first acts of the new government was to round up all the Christians and kill them. More than two-thirds of this pastor's congregation was executed in cold blood. He and his family fled to the United States with only the clothes on their backs. I wept after meeting this

EITHER GOD IS REAL, JESUS WAS IN FACT RAISED FROM THE DEAD, AND HEAVEN IS OUR ETERNAL HOME, OR WE'RE ALL JUST A BUNCH OF FOOLS CHASING SOME FANTASY TO SOOTHE OUR CONSCIENCES.

family because of the authenticity and depth of their faith. Instead of being cynical, they exhibited a humble spirit of gratitude and dependence on God.

In 1948, Richard Wurmbrand, a pastor in Romania, was walking to church when he was seized and imprisoned by the communist government. For eight and a half years his wife, Sabrina, and their son did not know where he was or whether he was dead or alive. When he was finally released, he discovered that Sabrina herself had been brutalized for three years in prison, and their nine-year-old son, Mihai, had been essentially orphaned. Yet, without hesitation, the two resumed their underground work.

> CHRISTIANITY IS, FOR THE MOST PART, NOT ABOUT WHAT HAPPENS IN THIS LIFE.

Soon thereafter, Richard was seized once again and sent back to prison for eight more years. Both he and his wife miraculously survived, and in 1965 they were released when Western churches paid a ransom to the government. The Wurmbrands moved to the United States, where they began to speak out on behalf of those suffering in communist hands. They eventually founded the organization known as Voice of the Martyrs.[2] Richard kept a journal of many of his moments in prison. The following account is both disturbing and challenging:

> We have had a very bad time lately. Our jailors have behaved worse than ever. They filled our bellies with water and jumped on us. They hung some of us up by our thumbs. They tied us with crossed arms between two pillars and whipped us until we fell over fainting.... If things continue like this, I shall not last long. I shall die. They will bury my corpse.... But to be dead is not possible for the human soul.... Sometimes I roar with laughter. I am not dead and never will be. "Whosoever liveth and believeth in me shall never die," said Jesus.[3]

ALL-OR-NOTHING TRUTH

Those types of testimonies bring our own trials into perspective, don't they? A man of God once offered me a golden nugget of counsel. He said, "Max, if what you teach or write about doesn't work in third-world or oppressed countries, then you can't teach or write about it here, because it's not biblical."

That statement might not be popular in today's materialistic societies or with the "health and wealth" preachers, but it's the truth.

Christianity is, for the most part, not about what happens in this life. We don't become Christians in order to gain a better standing in the community, to attain success in our careers, to fix our relationship problems, or even to experience God's healing. All of those things are simply potential by-products of our faith. They may happen; then again, they may not. The reason we become Christians is to find reconciliation with God, to be filled with His Spirit of peace, and to one day be with Him. I'm with Paul. If this faith isn't real, then we have been greatly deceived and are to be pitied.

BEFORE WE SEEK AND TRUST ANY FEELING OR EXPERIENCE, OUR FAITH MUST REST SOLIDLY ON THE TRUTH OF THE BIBLE.

There is nothing wrong with acquiring possessions and working hard to experience the best this life has to offer. But our greatest reward will never come to us in this life, but in the life to come. Our ultimate assurance is that we will one day overcome our final enemy, death. Paul continued in 1 Corinthians 15:20: "But Christ has indeed been raised from the dead." He goes on to declare, "Where, O death, is your victory? Where, O death, is your sting?" (v. 55). If we actually believe this, and if it is really true, then our loved ones are in paradise with God and our sorrows are temporary. It is also true that "our light affliction, which is but for a moment, is working for us a far more exceeding and eternal weight of glory" (2 Cor. 4:17 NKJV). Either it's all true or it's all a lie. There is no middle ground.

How does all this apply to winning the battle for the mind? When we experience periods of severe darkness, our feelings and our own limited perspectives will fail us. Only the knowledge of eternal truth will get us through. It is in times of deepest darkness that the mind comes under greatest attack. When Richard Wurmbrand's mind was under attack in prison, he wrote, "How trustfully a Christian can watch himself losing his mind, the inner tempest, the doubts, the moments of despair! Here, only truth counts. You struggle to find it, and only the ultimate, eternal truth survives."[4]

When we, like Richard Wurmbrand, find ourselves in the darkness of persecution, grief, abandonment, or financial pressure, and as the darkness squeezes in around us and threatens to suffocate our faith and life, the battle for our minds intensifies. To win this battle and to thrive on the jagged edge, we must understand what's happening. Either our faith is real or it's not. If it isn't real then we are fools for playing the game. If it *is* real, then why are we playing games?

MOST DEFINITELY REAL

For many years, even though I was a Christ follower and attended seminary, I was plagued by serious doubts. I searched for more than twenty years for a rational basis for my faith. My search included studying the arguments of highly respected scientists, thoughtfully considering well-documented and verifiable accounts of miraculous events, and interviewing many people who had personally experienced what only the power of God could explain. Then there were also the events in my own life that I can only describe as direct interventions of God. I've written in other books about some of these accounts. It's important to note, however, that before we seek and trust any feeling

SATAN'S MOST EFFECTIVE WEAPON MAY BE OUR OWN APATHY TOWARD SPIRITUAL WARFARE AS WELL AS OUR TENDENCY TO LIVE AS IF HE DOESN'T EXIST.

or experience, our faith must rest solidly on the truth of the Bible. Experiences can often be deceiving; we cannot depend on subjective experience to stimulate us or to validate our faith. God will sometimes perform a miraculous intervention, but He never does so simply to satisfy our curiosity. God calls us most of the time to believe, having not seen (see John 20:29).

DIVINE CONFIRMATION

Experience can provide a strong confirmation of God's activity. Three specific events have occurred in my life that confirm God's presence and guidance. I have a friend who is an atheist. He and I have engaged in an ongoing dialogue about God for several years. He is highly intelligent and skeptical, with degrees in engineering and architecture. Yet, he agrees, as do I, that the events I am about to describe go beyond human explanation.

GOD'S GUITAR

The first miraculous occurrence took place when I was an undergraduate at the University of Mississippi. I was at that time a pretty decent guitar player. During one monthlong semester break, I stayed alone on campus.

While I was praying one day, I sensed a still, small voice speaking to me and telling me to give away my guitar. I thought it strange, and at the time it didn't make much sense. But over the next couple of weeks, I continued to hear the message. I began to wonder if it might be God speaking to me. Within a few days, a name popped into my head, the person to whom I was to give my guitar.

When school resumed, I met with him and said, "You may think I'm crazy, but God told me to give you my guitar." Then I handed it to him. I expected him to look at me as if I was from another planet. Instead, he began to weep. He pulled from his backpack a journal, flipped to a certain page, and asked me to read it. He had written these words while praying in church over the break. "There is a guitar, which I, the Lord God, am going to give you. Though you do not know how to play, I will teach you to play and sing praises to Me."

WHAT OUR MIND PRODUCES ALSO DETERMINES THE PATH OF OUR ACTIONS AND ATTITUDES.

Through the years I've reviewed that experience over and over in my mind. I've tried to analyze all the angles that might identify this experience as a coincidence. Each examination leaves me more convinced than ever that it was a work of God. It was just too specific to be anything else.

LAWRENCE, KANSAS

The second event was nearly as strange as the first. For the first few years after finishing seminary, instead of leading a church or writing for a living, I found myself working as a United Parcel Service (UPS) truck driver in Tulsa, Oklahoma. It was a great job with a great salary and benefits.

One night during this period, I had a vivid dream—more vivid than any other dream I had ever experienced. In it, I was pastor of a small church in Lawrence, Kansas. The most intriguing aspect of this dream was that I had never been to Lawrence, Kansas. Neither did I have any connection to that place.

As soon as I woke up, I pulled out an atlas and located Lawrence. A burden instantly began to form in my heart for that town. Over the next week, the dream and Lawrence were all I thought about. I couldn't get them out of my mind.

When I finally couldn't take it any longer, I called my pastor and set up an appointment to meet with him for breakfast the following Monday. During our breakfast I told him about my dream and this strange burden I was carrying for Lawrence.

Then I asked if he thought God was telling me to go there to start a church. He wisely said, "I don't know, but time will tell. I do want to see us get a church started in Kansas City, though."

"No, Pastor," I said. "The dream was specific. It was Lawrence, Kansas."

My pastor was at that time our denomination's overseer for several states, including Kansas. Later that same week, he received a curious letter in the mail from a new church, requesting a charter with our denomination. The letter also asked my pastor if he knew of anyone who would possibly be interested in being their pastor. The church was located in— you guessed it—Lawrence, Kansas.

My pastor forwarded me the information, and within hours, the specifics of God's call began to come together. Three weeks later I was living in Lawrence, Kansas, serving as pastor of a church similar to the one in my dream. Could this have been a mere coincidence? It seems highly unlikely.

JESUS SAVES

There is one more account I need to share with you, one I've never before shared publicly. This one ties directly to the battle for our minds.

Shortly after committing my life to Christ—when I was youthful in body, long on zeal, and short on wisdom—I decided I was going to deliver the truth of God's Word to a group of satanists that was conducting rituals in a nearby neighborhood. To tell you the truth, at that time in my life I was probably moved more by a fascination with the supernatural than I was by compassion. Instead of simply reading and studying the Bible, I decided to read up on satanism. I naively visited the city library where I checked out a dozen books on satanism, witchcraft, and the occult. Back at home in my room, I began to skim through the volumes. I eventually closed the particular book I was reading, stacked it on top of the others on the floor, and then crashed on the bed for a little nap.

> A STRONGHOLD IS A PATTERN OF THINKING THAT BECOMES SO EMBEDDED THAT IT BINDS US AND MAKES US UNABLE TO EXPERIENCE GOD'S BEST IN THAT PARTICULAR AREA OF OUR LIVES.

As I lay there that afternoon, drifting in and out of sleep, I heard a high-pitched hum coming from the corner of my ceiling. When I turned my head to see what the noise was, an invisible force took hold of me. It seemed to be trying to suffocate me. I thrashed about on the bed as I wrestled with the unseen force. It suddenly occurred to me that the only one who could help me was Jesus, so I screamed "*Jesus!*" at the top of my lungs. The force instantly departed, and calm came over me. I sat up in bed drenched in sweat and completely drained of energy. I felt as if I had just competed in a wrestling match. Physically and emotionally shaken, I picked up the phone and called the lady I refer to as my "spiritual mom." She called the church office and then, along with one of the pastors, rushed to my house. After I described to them what had happened, the pastor observed the books on my floor, shook his head, and said, "When you read these books, you opened your mind up to Satan, and a demon jumped on you."

We prayed through the house, and the pastor returned the books to the library when he left. For days afterward, I walked around in a daze, saying to myself over and over, *It* is *real. It really* is *real.*

As I reflect on this event, what strikes me more than anything is the timing involved. Until that point in my life I had never experienced anything remotely similar to it. Was it mere coincidence that the afternoon I experienced this demonic attack was the very afternoon that I had been polluting my mind with those satanic books? Hardly. No, my friend, this thing is real.

If God is real and Jesus is in fact raised from the dead, then we must take seriously all of His teachings.

Most religions acknowledge Jesus as a great moral leader and spiritual teacher, but nothing more. But if Jesus was not exactly who He claimed to be—God in the flesh—then He wasn't a great teacher. He would have been an outright fraud. If any modern-day leader were to make the claims Jesus did, proclaiming himself to be God in the flesh and the only way to salvation, we would dismiss him as a madman. But if Jesus is who He claims to be, then He is not just a great teacher. He is Lord, and we must take seriously all of His teachings, including those about the existence and work of Satan.

> ᴄ⸙
>
> WHEN THOUGHTS ENTER OUR MINDS, IT IS OUR RESPONSIBILITY TO COMPARE THEM TO WHAT WE KNOW TO BE TRUE.

Jesus talked much about Satan. When tempted in the desert for forty days, Jesus didn't appeal to mind over matter or positive thinking to resist the temptation. He instead recognized the source of His temptation as Satan and rebuked him (see Matt. 4:1–11).

When He told the parable of the sower, Jesus compared the seed to the Word of God and the soil to our hearts. He said, "The farmer sows the word. Some people are like seed along the path, where the word is sown. As soon as they hear it, Satan comes and takes away the word that was sown in them" (Mark 4:14–15). When Jesus spoke to Simon Peter, He said, "Simon, Simon, Satan has asked to sift you as wheat. But I have prayed for you, Simon, that your faith may not fail" (Luke 22:31–32).

After Jesus ascended to heaven and sent back the Holy Spirit, the apostles picked up where Jesus left off. When confronting Ananias and Sapphira, who had lied about their donation of proceeds from a real-estate deal, Peter said to them, "How is it that Satan has so filled your heart that you have lied to the Holy Spirit?" (Acts 5:3). Satan actually tempted them to lie to God Himself.

Satan is a major player throughout the Bible. If we believe that God is real and that Jesus is His Son, the Messiah, then we must take seriously Satan and spiritual warfare. Paul warned us to stay alert, so that "Satan might not outwit us. For we are not unaware of his schemes" (2 Cor. 2:11). Did you get that? Satan has schemes and is trying to outwit us. When I read this passage, I visualize a four-star general studying a map of his territory, planning and strategizing when and where to deploy his troops. Satan is not omnipresent like God, but he has a military-style "command and control" system at work in the world. Satan himself rarely attacks us directly. He most frequently influences us by his world system and by his workers within that system. We must never forget that there is an actual enemy working behind the scenes to defeat us. It's real. There are unseen battles continually taking place all around us.

After the prophet Daniel had fasted and prayed for twenty-four days concerning Israel, an angel appeared to him. He touched Daniel and said, "Since the first day that you set your mind to gain understanding and to humble yourself before your God, your words were heard, and I have come in response to them. But the prince of the Persian kingdom resisted me twenty-one days. Then Michael, one of the chief princes, came to help me, because I was detained there with the king of Persia" (Dan. 10:12–13).

Yes, there is a spiritual war raging, and, just like Daniel, we are in the thick of it. Satan's most effective weapon may be our own apathy toward spiritual warfare as well as our tendency to live as if he doesn't exist, as if spiritual warfare is neither real nor relevant.

Ephesians 6:12 makes it clear that the war is real and certainly relevant. "For our struggle is not against flesh and blood, but against the rulers, against the authorities, against the powers of this dark world and against the spiritual forces of evil in the heavenly realms." It can't be stated any plainer than that. Our struggle in life is in part due to a

wrestling match with spiritual forces, and the primary way that demonic forces attack us is through
our minds. It's worth noting that my memorable
demonic encounter was the result of my opening
my mind to satanic influences. The battle really is
for our mind. Those who thrive on the jagged edge
must diligently protect their minds from attack and
invasion.

It all starts in our minds. God, the ultimate
thinker, is the mind behind creation. "God said, 'Let
there be light,' and there was light" (Gen. 1:3).
Everything originated from God's mind. He
thought and spoke, and things happened. God created man in His image, and one of the things that
sets humans apart from animals is our minds. People
are self-aware and creative, with free will and the
capacity for relationship. When a person dies, his
body goes back to dust, but his mind and soul live
on. In Deuteronomy 10:12, Moses urged Israel to
"serve the LORD your God with all your heart and
with all your soul." Throughout the Bible, the heart
and the soul are linked. The Hebrew word for heart
is *lebe*, which means the "mind" or "intellect."[5] The
heart of our soul is our mind. What our mind produces also determines the path of our actions and
attitudes. Our minds are under attack because the
Enemy knows that if he can bind our minds and con-
fuse us, he can greatly hinder our relationships with

God and render us ineffective in life. Paul said, "The god of this age has blinded the minds of unbelievers" (2 Cor. 4:4). And the god of this age doesn't just blind the minds of unbelievers, he also seeks to blind ours as well.

STRONGHOLDS

When the battle for our minds begins, it starts with a barrage of destructive philosophies, thoughts, suspicions, doubts, and fears. The Enemy's goal is for those thoughts to take root and to become strongholds in our minds that determine our actions. A stronghold is a pattern of thinking that becomes so embedded that it binds us and makes us unable to experience God's best in a particular area of our lives. Just to name a few, we can have strongholds of lust, depression, fear, cynicism, bitterness, poverty of spirit, unforgiveness, anger, and insecurity.

Strongholds begin as small seeds, single thoughts planted in our minds. Over time, if these seeds are not weeded out, they take root and grow into full-fledged vices that dominate us. Stronghold seeds take root in a variety of environments, from growing up in a destructive home, to an abusive marriage, to the devastation of the loss of a child, to the enticement of our own fleshly cravings. The good news is that we don't have to live in the bondage these strongholds create. We have the power to demolish them! "For though we live in the world, we do not wage war as the world does. The weapons we fight with are not the weapons of the world. On the contrary, they have divine power to demolish strongholds. We demolish arguments and every pretension that sets itself up against the knowledge of God, and we take captive every thought to make it obedient to Christ" (2 Cor. 10:3–5).

The way we demolish strongholds is by taking captive every thought and bringing it into submission to Christ. In other words, we must test everything to see if it lines up with what Christ has said. When thoughts enter our minds, it is our responsibility to compare them to what we know to be true. That's how we discern truth from falsehood. We look to what Jesus taught. After all, Jesus is the Truth. He said, "I am the way and the truth and the life" (John 14:6). On the other hand, Jesus described Satan as "a liar and the father of lies" (John 8:44). Strongholds bind, but truth sets free. Jesus told the disciples, "If you hold to my teaching, you are really my disciples. Then you will know the truth, and the truth will set you free" (John 8:31–32). Freedom comes by immersing ourselves in truth.

Our minds are like supercomputers. God made them this way for a reason. We have the remarkable ability to store information and then recall that information whenever we need it. Because of the way our minds are made, we can access truth to counter a false claim. But if we do not download the correct information and only download junk, there will be nothing of value for our "computers" to access.

Regardless of what our emotions tell us, we must fill our minds with what God says, because our emotions are not always reliable. The Lord said in Isaiah 55:8, "For my thoughts are not your thoughts, neither are your ways my ways." Proverbs 14:12 tells us, "There is a way that seems right to a man, but in the end it leads to death." We can't count on what our feelings tell us. It's imperative for us to check our thoughts in light of God's eternal truth. The way we do this is to know what God's Word says. We must "study to shew [ourselves] approved unto God ... rightly dividing the word of truth" (2 Tim. 2:15 KJV).

You may be going through a time of darkness in your life. It might not be a literal prison of torture and persecution, like the one Richard Wurmbrand experienced, but you are definitely being tortured in your mind. Your faith and sanity are under attack, and the darkness is threatening to engulf you. You don't have to let the Enemy destroy you or your faith. It's on this battleground of our psyche that we win or lose the war against Satan and his system to keep us bound by strongholds. What Richard Wurmbrand did in his prison, you can do in yours. Let God's eternal truth demolish the strongholds in your life and set you free.

NOURISHING
THE SOUL

*The great malady of the twentieth cen-
tury, implicated in all of our troubles
and affecting us individually and
socially, is "loss of soul." When soul is
neglected, it doesn't just go away;
it appears symptomatically in
obsessions, addictions, violence,
and loss of meaning.*

—THOMAS MOORE

In 1871 it all came crashing down. Everything
was a total loss. Years of investing, planning, and
hard work were gone in an instant, in a puff of

smoke—literally. Attorney Horatio Spafford had amassed a great fortune from his real-estate invest-ments on the shores of Lake Michigan. But the great Chicago fire of 1871 wiped out his holdings, leaving him mired in debt and on the verge of bankruptcy.

IT IS WELL

It was such a stressful time that Mrs. Spafford's health began to fail. By 1873, her health had declined so much that her physician advised her to take a trip to ease the stress. Horatio, Mrs. Spafford, and their four daughters had planned a long family vacation to Europe, but a last-minute business concern forced Horatio to delay his depar-ture. His wife and daughters sailed without him on the ship *Ville du Havre*.

Spafford's plan was to catch up with them in Europe, but that never happened. In the darkness of night on rough, stormy seas, the *Ville du Havre* collided with another ship and sank. Amid churn-ing waves and high winds, Mrs. Spafford watched in horror as her daughters were swept away to their deaths. As she struggled in the water, a falling mast knocked her unconscious. Amazingly, Mrs. Spafford's body snagged on a floating piece of wreckage, and she later revived and was rescued, along with a few others. She cabled from Europe two words to Horatio: "Saved alone."

Spafford immediately set sail to meet his wife in Cardiff, Wales. He asked the captain to take the same route his family's ship had taken. All the way his heart ached, and in agony he cried out to God.

When the ship arrived at the site of the tragedy, Horatio leaned over the ship's rail and gazed at the spot where his daughters' lives were lost. He began to pray. A great peace overwhelmed him, in the midst of which, he penned the following words:

IF YOUR SOUL IS WELL NOURISHED, YOUR LIFE WILL BE FULL OF THE FRUITS OF THAT NOURISHMENT.

> When peace, like a river,
> attendeth my way,
>   When sorrows like sea billows roll;
>   Whatever my lot, Thou hast taught me
> to say,
>   It is well, it is well, with my soul....
>
> But, Lord, 'tis for Thee, for Thy coming
> we wait,
>   The sky, not the grave, is our goal;

Oh trump of the angel! O voice of the
Lord!
Blessed hope, blessed rest of my soul![1]

These words became the beloved hymn "It Is
Well with My Soul," which throughout the decades
has been a source of inspiration to millions.

How could a man who had lost all his invest-
ments and his four daughters possibly have written
such words? How could he
have such peace when so
many others in equally desperate situations do not?

IF WE NOURISH OUR
SOULS, WE WILL BE
GOD-CENTERED AND
WILL FIND POWER
AND STRENGTH IN
TIMES OF NEED.

During the Great De-
pression of the 1920s and
'30s, many of those who lost
everything committed sui-
cide. Instead of ending his
life, Horatio Spafford experienced "peace like a river."
How could that be?

Could it be that Spafford's soul was nourished
by and centered on God—on whom he had laid a
foundation so that he had something on which to
draw in his time of need? Spafford undoubtedly
experienced all the pain, grief, and questions that
go along with deep personal trauma. Yet in the
midst of such a storm, God kept Horatio Spafford

safe by His supernatural peace because Spafford's soul was full of the Holy Spirit who swelled to the surface in his time of need. Within his being resided a reservoir of power.

GUARD YOUR HEART

Proverbs 4:23 declares, "Above all else, guard your heart [or soul], for it is the wellspring of life." When I was young I loved to visit my grandmother's house. She lived in a small country town, and in the middle of town was a natural spring. Pure, sparkling, refreshing water bubbled up from deep below the ground. Each time we visited, my dad would bring two or three empty milk jugs, and we would go down to the spring and fill them. That same spring is the source for a bottled-water company that ships natural spring water all over the United States.

Your soul is also a spring. Whatever is in you bubbles up and out, affecting your life. If your soul is well nourished, your life will be full of the fruits of that nourishment. But if your soul is malnourished, your life will reflect that malnutrition. That's why Proverbs says, "Above all else,"—first, before anything else—"guard your heart [soul]." Take care of your soul. Protect your soul. Feed your soul. Nourish your soul! The apostle Peter said it another way:

> Make every effort to add to your faith
> goodness; and to goodness, knowledge;
> and to knowledge, self-control; and to
> self-control, perseverance; and to perse-
> verance, godliness; and to godliness,
> brotherly kindness; and to brotherly
> kindness, love. For if you possess these
> qualities in increasing measure, they will
> keep you from being ineffective and
> unproductive in your knowledge of our
> Lord Jesus Christ.... For if you do these
> things, you will never fall.... So I will
> always remind you of these things, even
> though you know them and are firmly
> established in the truth. (2 Peter 1:5–8,
> 10, 12)

In other words, make it a priority to keep your
soul fed and focused on the right things. If you do,
you will never fall.

It is often easy for us to neglect the basics of the
faith because we are too busy or we think we already
know them. I know a man who went way off base in
his life because he regarded the basic truths of
Christianity as too simple. He was forever trying to
discover deeper, more profound revelation about
God, often going beyond the plain truths of
Scripture. Consequently, he's been through two

divorces, battles depression, and drinks heavily. Peter warned his readers to stick to the basics "even though you know them and are firmly established in the truth." If we do, we "will never fall." What a powerful promise! Notice, Peter did not promise that we would never have difficulty. He just said that we would never fall.

If we nourish our souls, we will be God-centered and will find power and strength in times of need. There is no peace on earth like the peace that comes when our souls are properly nourished and focused on God. Nourishing our souls requires faith and the discipline of appropriate choices, but it's the most important pursuit we can undertake for ourselves as well as for those we love.

It is not selfish to nourish your soul. It is only through a nourished soul that we can become an oasis of nourishment for others. What bubbles up from within our souls will spill over to those around us. And because what's bubbling out of us is natural and not contrived, people will be drawn to us and to God's Spirit in us.

> LIKE A LILY, WE NEITHER TOIL NOR STRAIN, YET WE GROW, EVEN THROUGH PAIN, INTO WHAT GOD DESIRES US TO BE.

When our souls are properly nourished, we don't have to try to be someone we're not, and we don't have to prove anything. We stop trying to give something we don't have. We just are who we are. Our lives cease to be defined by endless activities (religious or not) that we feel we "should" do to be right with God. Instead, we know God personally; we don't just know *about* Him. He's with us every day, and everywhere we go. The supermarket becomes as sacred as the chapel. We still participate in organized religious traditions, perhaps more than ever, but they take on new meaning. We are not doing them out of a sense of obligation, but out of thanksgiving. Like a lily, we neither toil nor strain, yet we grow, even through pain, into what God desires us to be (see Luke 12:27).

ONE OF THE GREATEST TRAGEDIES OF OUR MODERN SOCIETY IS OUR ADDICTION TO DISTRACTION.

Whoever you may be, regardless of your station in life, *now* is the time to begin nourishing your soul. You may be a Christian who has lapsed into cynicism or just plain apathy. It matters not what is in your past. Christ calls us to start afresh. We're never too old or too young to begin. But if we are to thrive on the jagged edge of life, we must not put it off. God has a unique plan for each of us that begins with Himself. Don't delay. Life is fleeting.

Jesus said, "I have come that [you] may have life, and that [you] may have it more abundantly" (John 10:10 NKJV). Are you truly experiencing that abundant life, or are you merely going through religious motions? Is Christ the Lord of your life? Is He your best friend? Psalm 40:2–3 says, "[The Lord] lifted me out of the slimy pit, out of the mud and mire; he set my feet on a rock and gave me a firm place to stand. He put a new song in my mouth." God desires to lift us out of our slimy pits and muddy ruts and put a new song in our mouths! What song is that? It's the song that comes from being right with God and having a nourished soul.

To atheists and nonbelievers I would say, "Hey, if I'm wrong about my faith, I haven't missed out on *anything*. My life is filled with incredible joy and fulfillment. God has shown Himself real to me, but if you're wrong, you've lost *everything!*"

Are you ready, despite all of your questions, fears, and pain, to take the risk of faith? You can be right with God and then experience the fruits of soul nourishment. But you must first make the choice to begin the journey. When you do, I guarantee that God will meet you there.

THREE SOUL STARVERS

To nourish our souls and become God-centered people, we must first uncover what *starves* the soul, get rid of it, and refocus our lives on what's really important.

Soul Starver 1: Too Much Distraction

In his remarkable book *Tyranny of the Urgent,* Charles Hummel surmises that we habitually let the urgent take priority over the important. One of the greatest tragedies of our modern society is our addiction to distraction. We've become so busy running to and fro that we are constantly distracted from the most important things in our lives, beginning with our souls.

Technology has helped create more leisure time than ever for the average person. Even so, few of us complain about having too much time to spare. Something or someone constantly diverts us from slowing down and getting to know God, ourselves, and the people God has put in our lives. The fax machine and e-mail have made on-demand reports and responses the norm. We have access to ATMs, fast-food restaurants, microwaves, cell phones, and text messaging, all designed to save us time. Why, then, do we find ourselves with less and less downtime? The economy is flourishing, and while having money is a nice thing, it's certainly not the answer. Statistics reveal that the more money we make, the more debt and pressure we carry.

We can't blame all our distractions on society. A large portion of the problem is in us. We convince

ourselves that we are too busy, but we keep putting
ourselves in position to load ourselves with more
busyness. And since we're so busy, we don't have
the time to look at ourselves
honestly and address personal
issues. It's easier to be busy than
to deal with issues of the soul.
When we finally slow down
physically, our minds are often
still racing.

The choice to slow down and
quiet the mind requires the self-
discipline and confidence to say
no to the expectations of others,
and to say yes to simplifying our
lives. It's hard at first, and we
even feel guilty, but we soon
find that this is the right thing
to do. The choice to slow down
is the first step to a nourished
soul. As Elaine St. James wrote
in *Living the Simple Life*, "An
amazing thing happens when we
slow down. We start to get
flashes of inspiration. We reach a
new level of understanding and
even wisdom. In a quiet moment we can get an
intuitive insight that can change our entire life and

THE CHOICE TO
SLOW DOWN
AND QUIET
THE MIND
REQUIRES THE
SELF-DISCIPLINE
AND CONFI-
DENCE TO SAY
NO TO THE
EXPECTATIONS
OF OTHERS, AND
TO SAY YES TO
SIMPLIFYING
OUR LIVES.

the lives of the people around us."[2] The first step toward nourishing our souls is to slow down and focus on what's really important.

Christ told a parable about a farmer who went out to plant seeds. Some of the seeds were trampled and never had a chance to grow. Some of them took root and grew, but were choked by weeds. The weeds represent the things in life that constantly divert and choke out the things of God, keeping souls from nourishment. Jesus said, "The worries of this life, the deceitfulness of wealth and the desires for other things come in and choke the word, making it unfruitful" (Mark 4:19).

Too much distraction starves our souls and makes us unfruitful.

Soul Starver 2: Too Much Amusement

On the heels of distraction has come the age of amusement and entertainment. Past generations lived in survival mode. Most did not even know what leisure time was. My dad, for example, woke up every morning before daylight, milked the cows, and then went to school. After school, he milked the cows again until suppertime. On Saturday, he worked again. Finally, on Saturday night he got to go out with his friends. On Sunday, the whole family rested, like most of society did at that time. Life was harder, but in many ways simpler. Today we may have more *leisure* time, but we have less *quality* time. We fill our spare time with soul-starving amusements that so often suspend our minds.

There is certainly a place for amusement. There are times when the mind needs a break, and amusement is helpful. But that's usually not the problem for us. The problem is simply that we don't know how to be quiet and alone. We don't know how to renew our minds. Romans 12:2 instructs, "Do not conform any longer to the pattern of this world, but be transformed by the renewing of your mind. Then you will be able to test and approve what God's will is—his good, pleasing and perfect will." We can know God's will for our lives, but doing so requires getting still before God and renewing our minds. But we're afraid of silence.

IF WE OFFER TO GOD OUR TIMES OF BOREDOM AND INACTIVITY, THEY CAN BECOME TIMES OF BLESSING DURING WHICH GOD SPEAKS TO US AND UNLEASHES OUR CREATIVITY.

It's difficult to hear God with all the commotion and noise going on around us and in our heads. If we offer to God our times of boredom and inactivity, they can become times of blessing during which God speaks to us and unleashes our creativity. Unfortunately, the moment we feel bored it becomes easier to pop in a video or to engage in other amusements that rob us of time we could use for nourishing our souls. Just as we have a hard time saying no to people and commitments, we have an even harder time saying no to amusements.

THE MOST SUCCESSFUL AND FULFILLED PEOPLE TEND TO BE EXTREMELY BUSY, YET THEY ALWAYS HAVE ENOUGH TIME TO DO WHAT'S IMPORTANT.

If we want to hear what God is saying, we have to become still before Him and switch our minds into the listening mode. God prefers whispering to shouting. Here's Elijah's experience of listening to God: "Then a great and powerful wind tore the mountains apart and shattered the rocks before the LORD, but the LORD was not in the wind. After the wind there was an earthquake, but the LORD was not in the earthquake. After the earthquake came a fire, but the LORD was not in the fire. And after the fire came [the voice of the Lord in] a gentle whisper" (1 Kings 19:11–12).

Imagine for a moment that a rich uncle hands you a check for $86,400. Your eyes bug out and your jaw drops. You can't believe your good fortune. Then, just before you give your uncle a great big bear hug, he says, "You have one day, exactly twenty-four hours, to spend as much of that money as possible. You can spend it any way you wish, on any project you wish, but at the end of the time period, any money that is not spent, I get back." What do you think the average person would do if he or she had an opportunity like that? Most of us would get mind and body in gear trying to spend as much money as possible.

Did you know that every day, each of us receives exactly 86,400 seconds of time? We are free to spend those seconds any way we choose, but at the end of the day, they are gone—never to return. We never get another chance to live today, and there is no guarantee that we will have another tomorrow. How are you spending your seconds? Are you *spending* precious time on wasteful activities, or are you *investing* it in ways that nourish your soul and build up others?

The most common excuse we make for our lack of devotion to renewal and spiritual growth activities is not having the time. But let's get real. The average American watches thirty to forty hours of television every week! We're busy, but for most of us it's not as much a matter of time as it is a matter of priorities. The most successful and fulfilled people tend to be extremely busy, yet they always have enough time to do what's important. Most have developed strong time-management skills.

There is truth in such statements as "An idle mind is the Devil's workshop." We need focus. Our children need focus. Please don't misunderstand me. I'm not against having fun. The challenge is to fill our time with activities that nourish our souls and release our spirits instead of activities that starve our souls and fill our minds with garbage.

When our minds are amused and in a suspended state, we allow all types of soul-starving ideas to influence our intellect. We spend precious little time renewing our minds. The kind of renewal I'm talking about doesn't have anything to do with sitting in a room with our legs crossed and our palms upraised, saying "Om-m-m." You might take a walk or go for a jog. I like mountain biking. My soul opens up when I'm on the bike trail; my soul opens up when I work in the yard. My personal practice is to spend a little time each day reading God's Word and praying. At least a couple of times a week,

TOO MUCH STUFF SQUEEZES OUT OUR DEEPEST DESIRES AND LEAVES AN EMPTY SPOT IN OUR SOULS.

however, I have to get completely alone and really connect with God. On those occasions I usually go to the high-school track or a trail through the woods and I walk and talk to God, sometimes for two or three hours. Without fail, I come back renewed. In every place I've ever lived, God has given me a special place to retreat in Him. It's those special quiet times with God that have kept me going throughout the years.

Regardless of how you do it, it's vital that you find a consistent way to connect with God. Yes, it will sometimes require the discipline of getting quiet and saying no to amusement so you can hear that still, small voice of the One who wants to talk to you. Too much amusement starves the soul.

Soul Starver 3: Too Much Stuff

Stuff clutters. Stuff complicates. Stuff restricts. Stuff hinders. Stuff adds responsibility. Multitudes of people can't do what God is calling them to do simply because they have too much stuff.

One of the key words that frees the soul is *less*. When a rich young ruler came to Jesus, his soul was crying out to follow the Lord. Jesus told him to sell all his possessions and give the money to the poor, then he could follow Him. The young man hung his head and walked away, saddened. He couldn't let go of his stuff. It kept him from experiencing the unforgettable journey of the soul with Christ. I imagine that when the man went back home to all his stuff, it suddenly seemed rather dull.

Too much stuff squeezes out our deepest desires and leaves an empty spot in our souls. If you're pursuing a dream or a vocation just to get stuff and you ignore your soul, you may in the end have a beautiful house set on a hill, but you'll have a soul in the gutter. Year after year we hear of rich and famous people going in and out of drug rehab, changing spouses like musical chairs, fighting anorexia, or being jailed for stupid crimes like shoplifting. Some even commit suicide. And why is that? Because, after a lifetime of pursuing fame and all the things money can buy, they are still empty. They've discovered the hard way that stuff can't fulfill.

Howard Hughes left an estate of more than two billion dollars. Yet he spent the last ten years of his life as a recluse. Even with all his wealth, his life ended in great loneliness.

John Paul Getty accumulated somewhere between two and four billion dollars in the oil business. But his private life was a shambles. He married and divorced five times.

A recent newspaper article reported that the vast majority of lottery winners suffer from what is now being labeled "affluenza," a serious disorder caused by the sudden acquisition of wealth. American psychologist Jessie O'Neil lists a plethora of life-ruining problems these winners face: depression, self-absorption, rampant materialism, addictive/compulsive behavior, and damaged relationships. Lottery winners have even formed support groups to share horror stories. Ninety percent of major money winners, according to a recent survey, reported that the windfall had damaged relationships with siblings and other family members who expected everything from one-time gifts to lifetime support. The most extraordinary conclusion was that after six months, big-money winners were no happier than car-accident victims who had been partially paralyzed.[3] Money and stuff do not bring true wealth. True wealth is the product of a nourished soul.

I'm not saying the answer is to sell everything we have. Jesus doesn't ask everyone to do that. Jesus knew that for the rich young man, stuff was his real god. That's why He told him to sell everything.

Jesus wanted to see which master the young man would serve.

JUST AS A PHYSICAL TRANSFORMA- TION TAKES PLACE WHEN WE CHANGE OUR EATING AND EXERCISE PATTERNS, OUR SOULS TRANS- FORM WHEN WE CHANGE WHAT WE FEED THEM.

Having stuff is not bad. But the pursuit of stuff, for stuff's sake, starves the soul. To follow your soul's calling, you may have to do without some things, but you will experience such joy and fulfillment that you probably won't miss them. If you pursue your soul's calling, chances are you'll eventually be in a place to have nice things and really enjoy them because you'll have them; they won't have you. Paul said, "I have learned to be content whatever the circumstances. I know what it is to be in need, and I know what it is to have plenty. I have learned the secret of being content in any and every situation, whether well fed or hungry, whether living in plenty or in want. I can do everything through him who gives me strength" (Phil. 4:11–13). Paul's happiness didn't come from his stuff, but from his soul's connection to God.

I know a doctor who was once the extremely successful head of a thriving clinic. He loved his work and had an upscale home, a beautiful wife, and three wonderful children. Yet, his soul wasn't fulfilled. As time passed, the gnawing inside his soul grew more and more acute. He felt that God was calling him to start an inner-city clinic for the underprivileged. He knew that starting a clinic would require him to drastically cut back his hours, which would mean less income. It would also mean a sizable financial investment, which also meant a huge risk.

He took the idea before his family, told them what he felt God was calling him to do, and laid out the plan. He told them this was his heart's desire, but he wouldn't do it unless they were all in agreement. He assured them he would still provide for them, but the family would have to make some serious cutbacks. The first act of simplification would be to sell their expensive home located on the grounds of the country club. His family, after several days of thinking it over, agreed to the plan.

Who wouldn't salute this family? They didn't let the love of stuff keep them from God's best. To obey God and to fulfill our soul's calling may require us to change some things. We might have to downsize. We may have to take a risk. If we hold on to stuff, it won't happen. Too much stuff starves the soul.

THREE SOUL NOURISHERS

Soul Nourisher 1: Choose Soul Food

Each of us has the ability to choose whether we will be a victim or a problem solver. The way we choose to respond to our circumstances is up to us. Personal responsibility does not necessarily mean taking the blame for something; it means having the ability to respond, or "response-ability."

Choice is what makes humans unique and separates us from animals. God doesn't want robots. He wants a creation that will respond to Him. There can be no love without choice. This is one reason God doesn't just reveal Himself openly. God stays somewhat hidden because He wants us to seek Him, and only then to find Him. He leaves clues all around, evidence of His majesty. As we pick up one clue after another, God progressively reveals a little more of Himself. But each step requires the choice of faith. As time passes, our faith grows. As we stated earlier, without faith, it is impossible to please God. God wants us to search for Him and to know Him.

When Jesus taught, He often spoke in parables. I used to think He did so in order to illuminate a point. But that is not at all the case. Jesus spoke in parables often to *conceal* a point and to require His listeners to search for its meaning. Those who chose faith and searched would discover a pearl of great wisdom. But those who chose *not* to believe would walk away cynical and confused. Jesus veiled truth in His parables in an attempt to stimulate faith in His hearers.

Choice is one of the most powerful gifts God has given us. Nourishing our soul and becoming God-centered begins with choice. And choice begins in the mind, not the emotions. The mind is the seat of the soul. This is why the first step in feeding our souls begins with the mind—we choose with the mind to feed on good things.

ℭ

THE MOST IMPORTANT MOMENT OF YOUR LIFE IS THE MOMENT YOU ARE EXPE-RIENCING RIGHT NOW.

Look at a clock with a second hand. Watch thirty seconds tick by. It's not a long time, is it? Yet large corporations pay millions of dollars to advertise their thirty-second commercials. Why? How can they justify spending that kind of money for such short spots? It's because advertisers know that what we put before our eyes influences our behavior. Rarely will a company run an advertisement only once. The same spot will run over and over and over again. The repetition plants into our minds the message the advertiser is trying to get across. How many times have you

caught yourself singing some silly commercial jingle
as you went about your daily business? Better yet,

how many times have you used the
word *Coke* when you meant "soft
drink"? Or *Kleenex* when you meant
"tissue"? What we put before our
eyes affects our minds.

A comedian once said, "If you
eat fat and greasy food, you become
a fat and greasy dude!" It's true.
We are what we eat. Many of our
souls are malnourished because we
feed on a diet of junk food and negative input. We seldom, if ever, take
the time to let God cleanse us and
put into our soul a healthy diet.

Just as a physical transformation
takes place when we change our
eating and exercise patterns, our souls transform
when we change what we feed them. Let's consider
Romans 12:2 again, but from a slightly different
angle. "Do not conform any longer to the pattern
of this world, but be transformed by the renewing
of your mind."

I don't understand how it happens, but a supernatural transformation takes place when we renew
our minds in Christ. Neither do I understand how
a tiny seed planted in the ground grows into a

THE SOUL
BECOMES
FULL WHEN
WE SLOW
DOWN AND
ABSORB ALL
THE LITTLE
MOMENTS
EACH DAY.

mighty tree. God has placed life into it. Everyone has within his or her soul a seed of faith—a measure of faith. We all have the potential to grow a beautiful garden of satisfying fruit. It's part of bearing God's image. But before that seed can grow and produce fruit, it must first be planted, fed, and tended. Conforming to the world system requires no effort. Anyone can conform. It's like a garden. If we just let it go, there will be weeds everywhere. We'll never harvest the good fruit. Nothing will make sense.

Feeding on soul food, on the other hand, takes time. It takes a conscious decision and a resolve to connect. We have to unplug from the world system and plug into Christ, the power source. We can't do anything unless we are first connected to the source. Jesus said, "No branch can bear fruit by itself; it must remain in the vine. Neither can you bear fruit unless you remain in me. I am the vine; you are the branches. If a man remains in me and I in him, he will bear much fruit; apart from me you can do nothing" (John 15:4–5). We are in a partnership with God. Only God can cause the transformation and growth of the seeds, but we must do the tending, feeding, and watering.

Once upon a time, a country preacher bought an overgrown piece of land. There were vines everywhere, almost covering the trees. The thorns and thistles were so thick the preacher could hardly walk. But each weekend, he worked his land faithfully, cutting away all the unwanted excess, burning it, breaking up the ground, planting seeds, fertilizing, watering, and then tending the soil by keeping the weeds out. Days turned into weeks. Weeks turned into months. Soon, the farmer's garden began to produce a beautiful harvest. One day, a friend stopped by and said, "Preacher, God sure has blessed you with a fruitful piece of land."

YOU CAN'T OUTGIVE GOD.

To that, the preacher replied, "Yes, He has, but you should have seen it when God had it all to Himself!"

Feeding the soul and becoming God-centered takes time. It requires cultivation. What we feed on eventually becomes part of our personality. If we feed on the positive, the positive will influence us more than the negative aspects of life. We grow in our ability to discern the difference between truth and error. We become more Christlike. We are able to respond appropriately in trying situations. Feeding doesn't make us right with God. Only repentance and acceptance of Christ's provision on the cross do that. But feeding the soul enables greater spiritual growth. It's not a chore; it just becomes part of who we are. Feeding on soul food is important because it brings everything in life into perspective.

A balanced soul-food diet consists of the following:

- A simplified life, which frees time for feeding our souls

- Daily meditation on God's Word: "Blessed is the man who does not walk in the counsel of the wicked or stand in the way of sinners or sit in the seat of mockers. But his delight is in the law of the LORD, and on his law he meditates day and night. He is like a tree planted by streams of water, which yields its fruit in season and whose leaf does not wither. Whatever he does prospers" (Ps. 1:1–3).

- Ongoing application of Scripture: "Do not merely listen to the word, and so deceive yourselves. Do what it says. Anyone who listens to the word but does not do what it says is like a man who looks at his face in a mirror and, after looking at himself, goes away and immediately forgets what he looks like. But the man who looks intently into the perfect law that gives freedom, and continues to do this, not forgetting what he has heard, but doing it—he will be blessed in what he does" (James 1:22–25).

- Consistent prayer and fellowship with God (talking honestly with God): "Devote yourselves to prayer, being watchful and thankful" (Col. 4:2).

- Reading good, uplifting literature that stretches the mind

- Pondering inspired works of art and listening to inspired music

- Gleaning insight from the stories and teachings of others

- Spending time outside in nature, if possible

- Exercising and eating healthy foods

Soul Nourisher 2: Heeding the Moment

The most important moment of your life is the moment you are experiencing right now. Don't miss it by living in the past or yearning for the future. Many people are so caught up with their past that they can't see the now. Others are so focused on future events that they miss the blessings at hand. The soul becomes full when we slow down and absorb all the little moments each day. It's in these small fragments of time that God illuminates truth in our soul. We can't do without our soul-feeding times, but living in the precious present and giving heed to priceless small moments throughout the day waters the seeds we have planted.

A flight I recently took out of the Colorado Springs airport was delayed because of bad weather. I had already turned in my rental car, so I was stuck in that small airport for more than two hours. I had completed a speaking engagement and was emotionally wiped out, dog tired, and ready to be home. The last place I wanted to be was grounded at the airport. I made the choice, however, not to give in to frustration, but to heed the moment, be creative, and see how God would redeem this time. My first thought was to find somewhere quiet, where I could be alone and pray. Have you ever tried to find a quiet, secluded place in an airport? As I walked around, I noticed a long hallway and what appeared to be some conference rooms. When I started down it, I saw a sign that read "Chapel."

Great, I thought. A chapel would be a perfect place to find a little peace and quiet.

The small chapel reminded me more of a miniature waiting room in a doctor's office—complete with vinyl chairs—than it did a church, but it did

> AS WE NOURISH OTHERS, WE NOURISH OUR OWN SOULS.

have a cross and a small altar with a Bible. Still, it was quiet. I couldn't even hear the big jets outside.

As I sat there, I began to commune with God. I didn't have much to say, so I simply opened my soul to what He wanted to say to me. I flipped through the Bible and read a couple of verses. Nothing profound struck me; I was just trying to refocus my thoughts on God.

> HAVING A NOURISHED AND GOD-CENTERED SOUL IMPARTS TO US HIS POWER AND PEACE TO MAKE IT THROUGH THE MOST TRYING EXPERIENCES OF LIFE.

Then I noticed what looked like an open prayer journal on the end table. The airport had provided the journal for people to date and record their prayers. It was at least three inches thick, full of other people's prayers from all over the world. I began to read those prayers and got so caught up in them that I couldn't stop. This journal was better than a novel! The diversity of trials people were experiencing was amazing. And the most encouraging thing that jumped out at me was the faith that the majority of them displayed in their writings. Several had written notes of thanks for some pretty extraordinary answers to prayer. Still others expressed prayers of deep gratitude for God's sustaining grace through their difficult times.

The more I read, the more God's Spirit moved in my soul. By the time I reached the last prayer in the book, I was weeping. The hour I spent in that little airport chapel was life transforming. I entered to find a little peace and quiet, and God showed up in an awe-inspiring way! It all happened because I chose to heed the moment instead of just flipping through a magazine somewhere else. Do these experiences always happen? No. Most of the time, nourishing the soul is not quite so dramatic. The point is that God is prepared to speak to us if we will but give Him the opportunity.

Living in the moment brings inspiration to our souls. Ordinary days become extraordinary. When we walk in God's Spirit and nourish our souls, even mundane things like walking to the mailbox or getting stuck in an airport can become adventures.

Soul Nourisher 3: Seeding into Others

Have you ever wondered how Mother Teresa could live in Calcutta, the world's most impoverished city? Completely surrounded by diseased, malnourished, and dying people, she was utterly at peace and totally fulfilled. Did she ever miss living in a "normal" home, in a "normal" neighborhood, with a "normal" family? I don't think she did.

Mother Teresa was so fulfilled in her soul that she never really thought much about what she was missing. Her focus was on her relationship with God and meeting the needs of those around her. As she poured out what God had placed inside her, she received supernatural strength and peace from Him. That's the only way she could continue to do what she did year after year.

"You can't outgive God." I've heard that life-transforming statement many times, and I know it's true. The more you seed into the lives of others, the more the harvest will come back to you. The Bible confirms this truth. I love what Isaiah 58:10–11 says about investing ourselves in the lives of others. (In this particular passage I'm partial to the King James Version because of the elegant wording.) "And if thou draw out thy soul to the hungry, and satisfy the afflicted soul; then shall thy light rise in obscurity, and thy darkness be as the noon day: And the LORD shall guide thee continually, and satisfy thy soul in drought, and make fat thy bones: and thou shalt be like a watered garden, and like a spring of water, whose waters fail not."

This passage promises us that as we nourish others, we nourish our own souls. Our souls will find satisfaction even in times of drought and sorrow.

The story of Johan Eriksson is another amazing example of what it means to seed into the lives of others.

During the Holocaust, trainloads of Jewish children were arriving daily in Sweden; many Swedish families had agreed to take in children for the "duration of the war." Most of these children were malnourished, thin, and pale, with dark, sunken eyes. They carried no belongings except despondent expressions and identification tags around their necks.

One of the Swedes who offered his home was Johan Eriksson. When Johan learned of a nine-year-old boy named Rolf who needed a home, his heart was overcome with compassion. Since Johan was a devout Baptist, little Rolf had to adjust to the Baptist way of life. In the beginning, whenever he heard a knock at the door, the boy would dive under the covers or hide in a closet. Again and again, however, Johan showered him with love and assurance. Rolf soon gained weight, and the despondent gaze left his eyes. He even began to laugh again.

When the threat of a Nazi invasion seemed certain, Johan's workmates would say, "When Hitler comes, you will be in trouble with that Jew boy in your house." Johan would tighten his jaw, clench his fist, and say, "They'll never take him so long as I'm alive."

In addition to the Nazi threat, Johan also received pressure from his fellow church members.

They assumed Johan would try to convert the boy. When confronted, Johan's jaw would tighten again. The Swedish government had promised the Jewish refugee organization that the children's religion would be kept intact. Even though Rolf accompanied Johan's family to church, Johan went to great lengths to maintain Rolf's religious heritage. He saw to it that Rolf continued to learn his Jewish traditions, so that when he reached the proper age he prepared for and celebrated his bar mitzvah. When the war was over, Johan wanted to return to Rolf's parents a son who had been raised according to their wishes. After the war, however, Rolf's parents were never found. They had died along with millions of others in the concentration camps.

Rolf grew up, but the events of his past caught up with him and he suffered a mental breakdown. The authorities sought to place him in a mental institution, but Johan would not allow it. "He belongs here," Johan insisted. "This is his home." Johan slowly nursed Rolf back to mental stability and calmness. Rolf went on to live a successful life and never forgot the man who had planted into his life the seeds of unconditional love.

Neither did Rolf forget the Spirit of Christ that had emanated from Johan's life. Johan was also changed forever. Because he gave out of his own soul, his soul became full.[4]

Once we have cultivated our souls and they are producing fruit, that fruit may rot if it just sits. We have to begin to feed others and to plant the seeds of our fruit in their lives.

Having a nourished and God-centered soul imparts to us His power and peace to make it through the most trying experiences of life. That's how Horatio Spafford found peace in the midst of tragedy. A nourished soul enriches our day-to-day existence. Our soul is a wellspring of life. Be sure to nourish it.

Thrivers admit they
don't have all the
answers, but they
know the One who is
the answer.

11

THE COURAGE TO THRIVE

*Be of good courage, and he shall
strengthen your heart,
all ye that hope in the* LORD.

—PSALM 31:24 KJV

As I stated in chapter 1, thriving on the jagged
edge is not about external or superficial success. It's
about experiencing soulfulness despite life's most
difficult trials. Instead of simply getting through life
in survival mode, thrivers live amid the reality of
pain and unanswered questions while trusting God's
faithfulness, knowing His peace, and taking hold of

His supernatural staying power. Thriving on the jagged edge is not about denying reality. It's about responding to a lesser reality with a greater one— God's eternal truth.

Thrivers admit they don't have all the answers, but they know the One who is *the* answer. They may be victims of persecution and poor treatment, but they have chosen not to adopt the mentality of a victim. Instead, they pour their lives into others. They have looked into the mirror of their souls, taken an honest inventory, and found themselves lacking. But despite their limitations, they exude a refreshing confidence. Thrivers aren't independent or codependent, they're interdependent, understanding their desperate need for God and others, their inability to live life on their own. They may stumble, but they always manage to stumble to the foot of the cross. They've discovered the God whose name is Mercy, and now they cling relentlessly to the hem of His garment.

READERS' GUIDE

*for Personal Reflection or
Group Discussion*

READERS' GUIDE

Like every genuine believer, you have discovered the Christian life is not a rose-covered garden. Deep-rooted weeds and prickly needles threaten your appreciation of the roses' beauty and fragrance. In other words, adversities, trials, setbacks, disappointments, and pain creep into what would otherwise be a blissful life. However, you can rise above every negative set of circumstances and live not simply as a survivor but as a thriver. This valuable truth came to you clearly and powerfully as you read *Thriving on the Jagged Edge*.

The following questions are designed to help you internalize what you have learned. They will

embed each truth in your soul and strengthen your
relationship with God. But they will also help you
externalize what you have learned by motivating
you to comfort and coach others.

Reflect on the questions privately or invite a
group of friends to discuss them. Expect the Lord
to use you to minister to others.

Chapter 1: The Jagged Edge

1. What three circumstances do you believe have people on the jagged edge today?

2. The author insists we can actually thrive on the jagged edge. Why do you agree or disagree with this premise? If you agree, what do you think it takes to thrive on the jagged edge?

3. How can you turn an apparently tragic circumstance into an opportunity to minister to others?

4. What gives you hope in hard times?

5. How would you encourage someone who claims life is hopeless?

CHAPTER 2: THE MYTH OF THE "NORMAL" LIFE

1. The author believes struggles are a normal part of life. Have you helped a fellow believer handle his or her struggles? What did you do? What was the outcome?

2. Do you wrestle with the question, "If God truly loves me, why does He permit the pain I am experiencing?" What conclusion have you reached?

3. Why do you agree or disagree that Jesus promised His followers a trouble-free life?

4. What changes in attitude might a suffering Christian make to stop living as a victim of circumstances and start living as a victor over circumstances?

5. Have you known any severely tested Christians who brought joy to others? How do you explain such joy in the midst of pain?

CHAPTER 3: EMBRACING THE STRUGGLE

1. What does the author say it means to "embrace the struggle"? What do you believe it means?

2. Why do you agree or disagree with the philosophy expressed by the motto, "No pain, no gain"?

3. The apostle James wrote, "Consider it wholly joyful, my brethren, whenever you are enveloped in or encounter trials of any sort or fall into various temptations" (James 1:2 AB). Why is it significant that he used the word "joyful" rather than "happy"?

4. What difference, if any, do you see between fatalism and the belief that God works in all our circumstances?

5. What takeaway value does Helen Keller's life have for those who question God's fairness?

CHAPTER 4: TRUSTING GOD

1. What might you tell someone who feels God doesn't care about him or her?

2. How has God shown a personal interest
    in your struggles?

3. What are some practical benefits of
    knowing God is in control when the
    world seems to be out of control?

4. The author discusses after-death episodes
    in which individuals claim to have seen
    God, observed heaven, and returned to
    life. Do you think these episodes are
    credible? If not, how do you explain
    them?

5. The author wrote: "One who thrives is one who trusts in God's sovereignty even when he may not understand the whys or have the answers to God's apparent silence in those moments when we desperately long to hear His voice." How do you define "sovereignty"? Do you think it would be easier to trust God if He spoke to you in an audible voice? Why or why not?

CHAPTER 5: WHEN FEAR WHISPERS

1. What advice can you offer a believer who withholds his life from God because He fears God will make it unpleasant?

2. Psalm 37:4 promises God will grant the desires of our heart if we delight in Him. Have you always received what you desired? If not, how do you explain the promise found in Psalm 37:4?

3. Why are fear and faith mutually exclusive?

4. How can the fear of God be a healthy condition?

5. What four steps does the author outline to fearless faith and comforting peace? Which of these steps do you consider difficult? Why?

Chapter 6: From Disappointment to Reappointment

1. Which disappointments have you experienced: disappointment with your circumstances? disappointment with yourself? disappointment with others? disappointment with God? Which one was hardest to overcome? Why?

2. How do you think the apostle Peter felt when the risen Christ questioned his love for Him (see John 21:15–17)? How can a Christian be restored to a purposeful, joyful life after disappointing the Lord?

3. The author relates a story about Tessa. What significant lesson about disappointment did Tessa learn?

4. What evidence have you seen to indicate God may be more concerned about changing believers than changing their disappointing circumstances?

5. What does it mean to receive a divine reappointment? What reappointment might God have in store for you?

CHAPTER 7: THE JAGGED EDGE OF WAITING

1. Does it seem hard to wait on the Lord? Why or why not?

2. Do you agree or disagree that God is never in a hurry, but He is always on time? Explain.

3. What might God be accomplishing while we wait on Him for guidance or resolution to a crisis?

4. What biblical characters come to mind as examples of those who waited on God? Which character do you best relate to? Why?

5. What reasons might God have for allowing you to experience a hardship for a
   long time?

CHAPTER 8: WHEN EVIL APPEARS TO TRIUMPH

1. Adversity strikes every Christian at one
   time or another. Occasionally, tragedies
   crash upon us like hurricane-driven waves.
   How can we be sure at such times that
   God loves us? That He is all-powerful?

2. What brief message or loving action
   helped you cope successfully with an
   especially difficult situation?

3. Why does God allow evil to exist in the world?

4. In what ways have you seen God's power in your life, even during the most difficult circumstances? How has He found ways to bring good, even the smallest amount, out of your adversity?

5. Read Revelation 21:4. Using five or six words, tell what life will be like when God destroys evil ultimately and completely.

CHAPTER 9: THE BATTLE FOR OUR MINDS

1. How would you respond to a well-meaning Christian who claims a believer would not be sick or financially strapped if he or she just had enough faith?

2. What impact do you think affluence has made on the quality of Christianity in Western nations? Would persecution be beneficial or harmful? Why?

3. Why is it possible for a financially challenged Christian to be more materialistic than a wealthy Christian?

4. The author cites two occasions when he believed God revealed His will to him: once through a still, small voice and later in a dream. Why do you agree or disagree that God may communicate His will in these ways?

5. In what sense is the believer's mind a battleground? How can you win the battle for your mind?

CHAPTER 10: NOURISHING THE SOUL

1. The author relates the circumstances that led to the writing of the hymn "It Is Well with My Soul." What impressed you most about this story? Why?

2. The author writes: "Make it a priority to keep your soul fed and focused on the right things. If you do, you will never fall." What "right things" should a believer focus on?

3. How can technology aid your relationship with God? How might it damage it?

4. What steps might a believer take to reduce his or her busyness in order to devote more time to nourish the soul?

5. When is clutter a foe? If it is a foe, how should believers combat it?

Chapter 11: The Courage to Thrive

1. What would you say are a few essential differences between a survivor and a thriver?

2. What would you identify as the most valuable step you can take to help you thrive in the midst of difficulty?

3. Which of God's eternal truths must a person take to heart if he or she is to thrive?

4. How is it possible for a believer suffering a terminal illness to sincerely praise God? What about a person's life might make him or her able to do so?

5. With whom will you share the comfort and wisdom you gained from this book? When will you offer both?

NOTES

Chapter 1: The Jagged Edge

1. As quoted by Charles R. Swindoll in *Hope Again* (Dallas: Word, 1997), 12.
2. Elisabeth Kubler-Ross, *Life Lessons* (New York: Scribner, 2000), 25.
3. *Merriam-Webster's Collegiate Dictionary*, 11th ed., s.v. "transcend."

Chapter 2: The Myth of the "Normal" Life

1. M. Scott Peck, *The Road Less Traveled* (New York: Simon & Schuster, 1978), 15.
2. Richard Exley, *Strength for the Storm* (Nashville: Thomas Nelson, 1999), 3.

3. James Strong, *Abingdon's Strong's Exhaustive Concordance of the Bible* (Nashville: Abingdon Press, 1980), 37 of Greek Dictionary.
4. June Scobee Rogers, *Silver Linings* (Macon, GA: Peake Road Publishing, 1995), 35.

Chapter 3: Embracing the Struggle

1. Jessica McElroth, "African American History: Frederick Douglass Quotes," About, Inc., http://afroamhistory.about.com/od/frederickdouglass1/a/fdouglassquotes.htm.
2. William Shakespeare, *As You Like It*, act 2, scene 1, line 14.
3. Gary Fenchuk, *Timeless Wisdom* (Midlothian, VA: Cake Eaters, Inc., 1994), 142.
4. Margery Williams, *The Velveteen Rabbit* (New York: Doubleday, 1958), 5.
5. Helen Keller, *My Religion* (1927), quoted in Dale Carnegie, *Dale Carnegie's Scrapbook* (New York: Simon & Schuster, 1959), 114.

Chapter 4: Trusting God

1. Grant R. Jeffrey, *The Signature of God* (Toronto: Frontier Research Publications, Inc., 1998), 106, 114–15, 118–19.
2. Stephen C. Meyer, cited in Richard Swenson, *More Than Meets the Eye* (Colorado Springs: Navpress, 2000), 72.

3. Ibid., 72–73.
4. Doris Sanders, *Clover* (Chapel Hill, NC: Algonquin, 1990), 13.
5. Don Piper, *90 Minutes in Heaven* (Grand Rapids, MI: Revell, 2004).
6. Joni Eareckson Tada and Steve Estes, *A Step Further* (Carmel, NY: Guideposts, 1979), 86.

Chapter 5: When Fear Whispers

1. Stan Toler, *God Has Never Failed Me, but He's Sure Scared Me to Death a Few Times* (Colorado Springs: Honor Books, 1995).
2. Harry Emerson Fosdick, Words of Wisdom 4 U!, www.wow4u.com/fear-quotes.
3. Rick Warren, "What Your Fears Do to You," Home & Holidays, www.homeholidaysfamily-andfun.com/files2/viewarticle.php?articleid=9853.
4. John Steinbeck, *The Meaning of Persons* (New York: Harper Collins, 1957), 64.
5. Robert Frost, quoted in Donald O. Bolander, comp., *Instant Quotation Dictionary* (Mundelein, IL: Career Institute, 1969), 115.
6. *Merriam-Webster's Collegiate Dictionary*, 11th ed., s.v. "fear."
7. Strong, *Abingdon's Strong's Exhaustive Concordance of the Bible*, 76 of Greek Dictionary.

8. Mark Tabb, *Out of the Whirlwind* (Nashville: Broadman & Holman, 2003), 77.
9. Oswald Chambers, *The Highest Good*, cited in "Reflections: Classic and Contemporary Excerpts," *Christianity Today*, February 9, 1998, vol. 39.
10. John Ortberg, *If You Want to Walk on Water, You've Got to Get Out of the Boat* (Grand Rapids, MI: Zondervan, 2001), 147.
11. Henry Blackaby, *Experiencing God* (Nashville: Broadman & Holman, 1994), 233.
12. Ortberg, *If You Want to Walk on Water*, 82–83.

Chapter 6: From Disappointment to Reappointment

1. For this phrase and concept I am indebted to its originator, Joyce Meyer, who has graciously granted permission to use it.
2. The letters written by Tessa are used with her permission.
3. Joyce Meyer, *Managing Your Emotions* (Tulsa, OK: Harrison House, 1997), 145–46.

Chapter 7: The Jagged Edge of Waiting

1. F. B. Meyer, *Choice Notes on the Psalms* (Grand Rapids, MI: Kregel, 1984), 23.
2. Strong, *Abingdon's Strong's Exhaustive Concordance of the Bible*, 72 of Hebrew and Chaldee Dictionary.

3. Blackaby, *Experiencing God*, 30.
4. Jim Cymbala with Dean Merrill, *Fresh Faith* (Grand Rapids, MI: Zondervan, 1999), 111.

Chapter 8: When Evil Appears to Triumph

1. Epicurus, cited in www.philosophyofreligion.info/problemofevil.html ©2003–2006 Tim Holt, 1.
2. John Eldredge, *Epic* (Nashville: Nelson, 2004), 51–52.
3. Philip Yancey, *Disappointment with God* (Grand Rapids, MI: Zondervan, 1988), 71.
4. Heather Gemmen, *Startling Beauty* (Colorado Springs: Cook Communications, 2004), 58–64, 223–24.

Chapter 9: The Battle for Our Minds

1. John Foxe, *Foxe's Annals of Martyrs* (Burlington, ON: Inspirational Promotions, 1960), 33.
2. Richard Wurmbrand, *Tortured for Christ* (Middlebury, IN: Living Sacrifice Books, 1976).
3. Richard Wurmbrand, *If Prison Walls Could Speak* (Bartlesville, OK: Christian Missions to the Communist World, 1972), 105–6.
4. Ibid., 111.

5. Strong, *Abingdon's Strong's Exhaustive Concordance of the Bible*, 58 of Hebrew and Chaldee Dictionary.

Chapter 10: Nourishing the Soul

1. Horatio Spafford and Philip P. Bliss, "It Is Well with My Soul," The Cyber Hymnal, http://www.cyberhymnal.org/htm/i/t/i/itis well.htm.
2. Elaine St. James, *Living the Simple Life* (New York: Hyperion, 1996), 221.
3. "It's a Rich Man's World of Misery," *Herald Sun*, (Melbourne, Australia), June 11, 2001, 20.
4. Alan Loy McGinnis, *Bringing Out the Best in People* (Minneapolis: Augsburg, 1985), 176.

BIBLIOGRAPHY

Blackaby, Henry. *Experiencing God*. Nashville: Broadman & Holman, 1994.

Carnegie, Dale. *Dale Carnegie's Scrapbook*. New York: Simon & Schuster, 1959.

Chambers, Oswald. Cited in "The Highest Good." *Christianity Today*. February 9, 1998, vol. 39.

Cymbala, Jim, with Dean Merrill. *Fresh Faith*. Grand Rapids, MI: Zondervan, 1999.

Eldredge, John. *Epic*. Nashville: Nelson, 2004.

Exley, Richard. *Strength for the Storm*. Nashville: Thomas Nelson, 1999.

Fenchuk, Gary. *Timeless Wisdom*. Midlothian, VA: Cake Eaters, Inc., 1994.

Foxe, John. *Foxe's Annals of Martyrs*. Burlington, ON: Inspirational Promotions, 1960.

Gemmen, Heather. *Startling Beauty*. Colorado Springs: Cook Communications, 2004.

Herald Sun, Melbourne, Australia, June 11, 2001.

Jeffrey, Grant R. *The Signature of God*. Toronto: Frontier Research Publications, Inc, 1998.

Kubler-Ross, Elisabeth. *Life Lessons*. New York: Scribner, 2000.

McGinnis, Alan Loy. *Bringing Out the Best in People*. Minneapolis: Augsburg, 1985.

Meyer, F. B. *Choice Notes on the Psalms*. Grand Rapids, MI: Kregel, 1984.

Meyer, Joyce. *Managing Your Emotions*. Tulsa, OK: Harrison House, 1997.

Ortberg, John. *If You Want to Walk on Water You've Got to Get Out of the Boat*. Grand Rapids, MI: Zondervan, 2001.

Peck, M. Scott. *The Road Less Traveled*. New York: Simon & Schuster, 1978.

Piper, Don. *90 Minutes in Heaven*. Grand Rapids, MI: Revell, 2004.

Rogers, June Scobee. *Silver Linings.* Macon, GA: Peake Road Publishing, 1995.

Sanders, Doris. *Clover.* Chapel Hill, NC: Algonquin, 1990.

St. James, Elaine. *Living the Simple Life.* New York: Hyperion, 1996.

Steinbeck, John. *The Meaning of Persons.* New York: Harper Collins, 1957.

Strong, James. *Abingdon's Strong's Exhaustive Concordance of the Bible.* Nashville: Abingdon Press, 1980.

Swenson, Richard. *More Than Meets the Eye.* Colorado Springs: Navpress, 2000.

Swindoll, Charles R. *Hope Again.* Dallas: Word, 1997.

Tabb, Mark. *Out of the Whirlwind.* Nashville: Broadman & Holman, 2003.

Tada, Joni Eareckson, and Steve Estes. *A Step Further.* Carmel, NY: Guideposts, 1979.

Toler, Stan. *God Has Never Failed Me, but He's Sure Scared Me to Death a Few Times.* Colorado Springs: Honor Books, Cook Communications, 1995.

Williams, Margery. *The Velveteen Rabbit.* New York: Doubleday, 1958.

Wurmbrand, Richard. *If Prison Walls Could Speak*. Bartlesville, OK: Christian Missions to the Communist World, 1972.

———. *Tortured for Christ*. Middlebury, IN: Living Sacrifice Books, 1976.

Yancey, Philip. *Disappointment with God*. Grand Rapids, MI: Zondervan, 1988.

ABOUT THE
AUTHOR

Max Davis holds a bachelor's degree in journalism and a master's degree in biblical studies. He has served as a pastor, UPS truck driver, and coach. The author of five books, including the national best seller *Never Stick Your Tongue Out at Mama* (Bantam Doubleday Dell), Max now devotes his time to writing and speaking, including a seminar based on his books *Desperate Dependence* and *Thriving on the Jagged Edge*. He and his wife, Alanna, live outside Baton Rouge, Louisiana. They have three children and one spoiled poodle.

Max enjoys hearing from his readers, and he can be persuaded to leave home to speak at conferences, retreats, and churches. To contact Max, visit his Web site, www.MaxDavis.org, e-mail him at mdbook@aol.com, or write to him at 22083 Greenwell Springs Rd., Greenwell Springs, LA 70739.

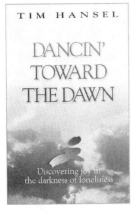

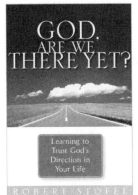
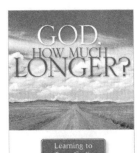

The Word at Work Around the World

A vital part of Cook Communications Ministries is our international outreach, Cook Communications Ministries International (CCMI). Your purchase of this book, and of other books and Christian-growth products from Cook, enables CCMI to provide Bibles and Christian literature to people in more than 150 languages in 65 countries.

Cook Communications Ministries is a not-for-profit, self-supporting organization. Revenues from sales of our books, Bible curricula, and other church and home products not only fund our U.S. ministry, but also fund our CCMI ministry around the world. One hundred percent of donations to CCMI go to our international literature programs.

CCMI reaches out internationally in three ways:

- Our premier International Christian Publishing Institute (ICPI) trains leaders from nationally led publishing houses around the world.

- We provide literature for pastors, evangelists, and Christian workers in their national language.

- We reach people at risk—refugees, AIDS victims, street children, and famine victims—with God's Word.

Word Power, God's Power

Faith Kidz, RiverOak, Honor, Life Journey, Victor, NexGen — every time you purchase a book produced by Cook Communications Ministries, you not only meet a vital personal need in your life or in the life of someone you love, but you're also a part of ministering to José in Colombia, Humberto in Chile, Gousa in India, or Lidiane in Brazil. You help make it possible for a pastor in China, a child in Peru, or a mother in West Africa to enjoy a life-changing book. And because you helped, children and adults around the world are learning God's Word and walking in his ways.

Thank you for your partnership in helping to disciple the world. May God bless you with the power of his Word in your life.

For more information about our international ministries, visit www.ccmi.org.

Additional copies of THRIVING ON THE JAGGED EDGE
and other Life Journey books
are available wherever good books are sold.

If you have enjoyed this book,
or if it has had an impact on your life,
we would like to hear from you.

Please contact us at:

LIFE JOURNEY BOOKS
Cook Communications Ministries, Dept. 201
4050 Lee Vance View
Colorado Springs, CO 80918

Or visit our Web site: www.cookministries.com